Algebra is Easy Part 1

Math is Easy Series
Book #1

Written By:
April Chloe Terrazas

Dedicated To:
Mom and Dad

I0141968

Use the following resources along with this book for MAXIMIZED practice and awesomeness!

*Algebra is Easy Part 1 SUCCESS BOOK
- matches page for page to Algebra is Easy Part 1 with extra practice problems plus answers.
- 2 tests per section (12 total) + answers.

*Algebra is Easy FULL BOOK WEBINAR
STEP-BY STEP EXPLANATIONS!
-videos of Algebra is Easy Part 1 page by page explained
-videos of Algebra is Easy Part 1 SUCCESS BOOK page by page explained

COMING in the Math is Easy Series
-Geometry is Easy
-Algebra 2 is Easy
-PreCalculus is Easy
-Elementary School Math is Easy
-Middle School Math is Easy
-The GED is Easy
-The SAT is Easy

*Algebra is Easy Part 2 + Workbook + Tests and Webinar

All resources (+ package deals!) available at www.Crazy-Brainz.com

Written by April Chloe Terrazas

Algebra Is Easy: Part 1
April Chloe Terrazas, BS University of Texas at Austin, Mathematics Tutor since 2004.

ISBN#: 978-1-941775-25-7
Visit us on the web! www.Crazy-Brainz.com

Cover design, illustrations and text by: April Chloe Terrazas

Table of Contents

More practice: Algebra Is Easy Part 1 SUCCESS BOOK (Workbook + Test Book)

You ARE AWESOME

Written by April Chloe Terrazas

Adding Negative Numbers

A. (- 3) + (- 4) = ?

Adding two negative numbers:
(just like adding two positive numbers)
the number gets LARGER.
Beginning on a number line at the point (-3) and add (-4), move in the negative direction (to the left) 4 spaces. Where do you end up?
At -7.

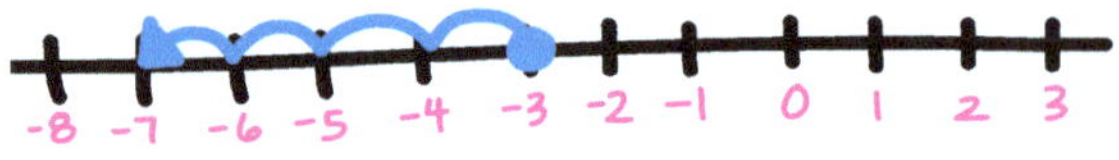

B. 3 + (- 4) = ?

Adding one positive and one negative number:
Beginning on a number line at the point (+3), then add (-4), move in the negative direction (to the left) 4 spaces. Where do you end up?
At -1.
You are actually SUBTRACTING.

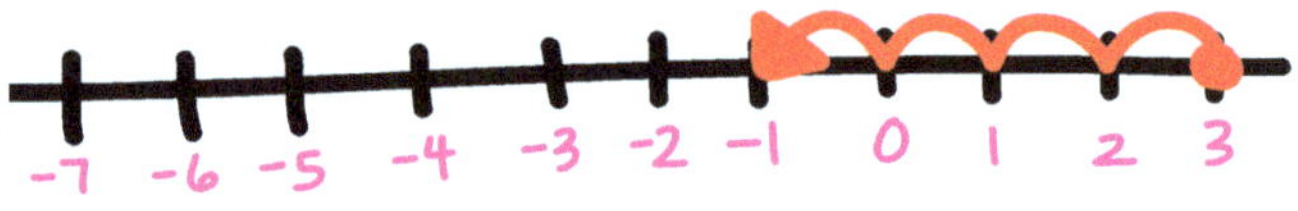

Tip: SAME SIGN ADD, DIFFERENT SIGN SUBTRACT.

Adding two negative (-) numbers, ADD THEM to make a LARGER negative number.

Answer is ALWAYS NEGATIVE when adding two negative numbers.

(-3) + (-4), same sign, add (3 + 4 = 7),

answer is negative because both are negative numbers and have been combined to make a larger negative.

Answer = - 7

Adding one positive (+) and one negative (-) number, SUBTRACT the smaller number from the larger number. The sign on the answer is the same as the sign of the larger number.

Answer can be EITHER POSITIVE OR NEGATIVE.

3 + (-4), different signs, subtract (4 - 3 = 1), answer is negative because the larger number (4) is negative.

Answer = - 1

Examples

A. (-3) + (-4) = -7

B. 3 + (-4) = -1

C. 9 + (-7) = 2
different signs, subtract, (9 - 7 = 2)
answer is positive because the larger number (9) is positive.

D. 6 + (-8) = -2
different signs, subtract, (8 - 6 = 2)
answer is negative because the larger number (8) is negative.

E. (-12) + (-1) = -13
same sign, add, (12 + 1 = 13),
answer is negative because both numbers are negative.

Adding Negative Numbers

Practice:

1. (-5) + (-8) =
(See ex. A or E for reference)

2. (-4) + 9 =
ex. B, C or D

3. 12 + (-19) =
ex. B, C or D

4. (-20) + (-30) =
ex. A, E

5. 18 + (-18) =
ex. B, C or D

6. 0 + (-6) =
ex. B, C or D

7. (-8) + 10 =
ex. B, C or D

8. (-4) + (-3) =

9. (-2) + 8 =

10. 9 + (-10) =

11. (-22) + (-33) =

12. 15 + (-15) =

13. 0 + (-7) =

14. (-6) + 12 =

Written by April Chloe Terrazas

Practice ANSWERS

1. (-5) + (-8) = -13

same sign, add, (5 + 8 = 13), answer is negative because both numbers are negative.

2. (-4) + 9 = 5

different sign, subtract, (9 - 4 = 5), answer is positive because larger number (9) is positive.

3. 12 + (-19) = -7

different sign, subtract, (19 - 12 = 7), answer is negative because larger number (19) is negative.

4. (-20) + (-30) = -50

same sign, add, (20 + 30 = 50), answer is negative because both numbers are negative.

5. 18 + (-18) = 0

different sign, subtract, (18 - 18 = 0), answer is zero, not positive or negative.

6. 0 + (-6) = -6

different sign, subtract, (6 - 0 = 6), answer is negative because the larger number is negative.

7. (-8) + 10 = 2

different sign, subtract, (10 - 8 = 2), answer is positive because the larger number is positive.

8) -7 **9) 6** 10) -1 **11) -55** 12) 0 **13) -7** 14) 6

Subtracting Negative Numbers

Treat "minus" and "negative" in the same way.

4 - 3 and 4 + (- 3) ARE THE SAME PROBLEM.
(Subtracting 3 and adding (-3) is the same)

4 - 3 = 1 Different signs, [positive 4 and negative 3], subtract	4 + (-3) = 1 Different signs, [positive 4 and negative 3], subtract

NEXT, If you see a minus sign NEXT TO a negative sign, **THEY BOTH BECOME POSITIVE.**
Minus negative - (-) is the same as plus positive + (+)

A. **3 - (- 2) is the same as 3 + (+ 2), same as 3 + 2 which equals + 5**.

B. **4 - (- 8) is the same as 4 + (+ 8), same as 4 + 8 which equals + 12**.

C. What if the *first number is NEGATIVE followed by - (-)?* - 7 - (- 3) = - 4
- 7 - (- 3) is the same as - 7 + (+ 3), which is the same as - 7 + 3
- 7 + 3, different signs, subtract (*rule from previous page*)
7 - 3 = 4, the answer is NEGATIVE because the larger number (7) is negative,
so the final answer is NEGATIVE FOUR. (- 4).

- 8 - (- 20) = 12

D. **- 8 - (- 20) is the same as - 8 + (+ 20), which is the same as - 8 + 20**
- 8 + 20, different signs, subtract (*rule from previous page*)
20 - 8 = 12, the answer is POSITIVE because the larger number (20) is positive
so the final answer is POSITIVE 12. (+ 12).

E. What if *first number is negative minus another number*? - 6 - 5 = - 11
- 6 and - 5 (negative and minus are the same), same sign, add (*rule from previous page*)
6 + 5 = 11, answer is NEGATIVE because both numbers are negative,
so the final answer is NEGATIVE 11. (- 11).

(+) = positive, (-) = negative

Examples

A. 3 - (- 2) = 5

B. 4 - (- 8) = 12

C. - 7 - (- 3) = - 4

D. - 8 - (- 20) = 12

E. - 6 - 5 = - 11

F. 8 - (- 5) = 13
same as 8 + (+ 5), 8 + 5 = 13
answer is POSITIVE because both numbers are (+).

G. - 7 - (- 4) = -3
same as -7 + (+ 4), which is -7 + 4
different signs, subtract, 7 - 4 = 3,
answer is NEGATIVE because larger number (7) is (-).

H. - 15 - 9 = - 21
same sign, add (15 + 9 = 21)
answer is NEGATIVE because both numbers are (-).

Subtracting Negative Numbers

Practice:

1. (-5) - (-8) =
See ex. C, D or G for reference

2. (-4) - 9 =
ex. E, H

3. 12 - (-19) =
ex. A, B or F

4. (-20) - (-30) =
ex. C, D or G

5. 18 - (-18) =
ex. A, B or F

6. 0 - (-6) =
ex. A, B or F

7. (-8) - 10 =
ex. E, H

8. (-2) - (-9) =

9. (-1) - 6 =

10. 15 - (-11) =

11. (-10) - (-20) =

12. 13 - (-13) =

13. 0 - (-8) =

14. (-4) - 16 =

Written by April Chloe Terrazas

Practice ANSWERS

1. (-5) - (-8) = 3

same as -5 + (+8), same as -5 + 8, different signs, subtract, (8 - 5 = 3), answer is positive because larger number (8) is positive.

2. (-4) - 9 = -13

same sign, add, (4 + 9 = 13), answer is negative because both numbers are negative.

3. 12 - (-19) = 31

same as 12 + (+ 19), same as 12 + 19, same sign, add, (12 + 19 = 31), answer is positive because both numbers are positive.

4. (-20) - (-30) = 10

same as -20 + (+ 30), same as - 20 + 30, different signs, subtract, (30 - 20 = 10), answer is positive because larger number (30) is positive.

5. 18 - (-18) = 36

same as 18 + (+ 18), same as 18 + 18, same sign, add, (18 + 18 = 36), answer is positive because both numbers are positive.

6. 0 - (-6) = 6

same as 0 + (+ 6), same as 0 + 6, same sign, add, (0 + 6 = 6), answer is positive because 6 is positive.

7. (-8) - 10 = -18

same sign, add, (8 + 10 = 18), answer is negative because both numbers are negative.

8) 7 9) -7 10) 26 11) 10 12) 26 13) 8 14) -20

Multiplying & Dividing #'s & Variables

The symbols: *, $\cdot$, x, #(#) all = multiply

A. $3 * 4 = 3 \cdot 4 = 3 \times 4 = 3(4) = 12$
B. $5 * a = 5 \cdot a = 5 \times a = 5(a) = 5a$
C. $x * y = x \cdot y = x \times y = x(y) = xy$

Note: Examples B, C, E, F, I, J, M and N cannot be simplified any further because of the variable. 5 times a = 5a.

When a number is directly next to a variable, like "5a", this means they are being <u>multiplied</u>.

$5(a) = 5a$ $\quad$ $200(y) = 200y$

$10/x = 10/x$ $\quad$ $x \div 12 = x/12$

÷ or / = division

Fraction = Division

D. $10 \div 2 = 10/2 = 5$
E. $8 \div x = 8/x = 8/x$
F. $x \div y = x/y = x/y$

<u>Multiplying & Dividing (+) and (-) #'s & Variables</u>

How to tell if the answer is positive (+) or negative (-):

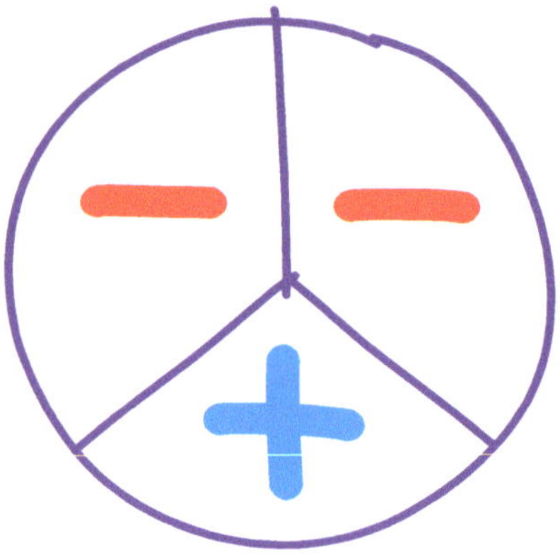

Use your finger to cover the signs of the two numbers in the problem.

Ex H: - 3 $\cdot$ 5, <u>cover one positive and one negative sign</u>, the section that is still showing gives you the sign of the answer. The section still showing in this example would be negative so the answer is negative 15. (- 15).

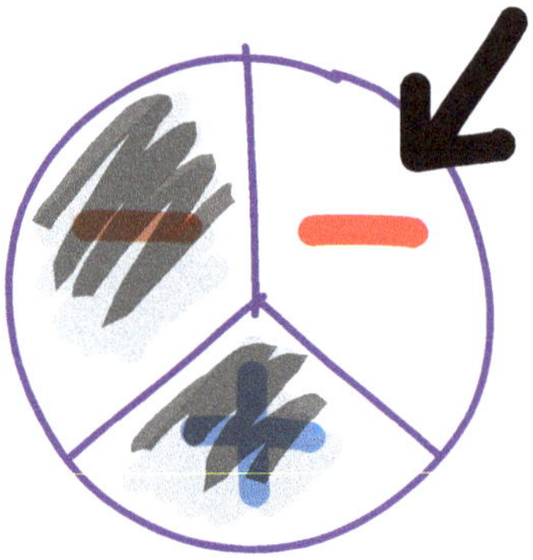

More examples:

G. (-3) x (-5) = + 15
H. (-3) $\cdot$ (5) = - 15
I. (-3) * y = - 3y
J. -3(-y) = + 3y

K. (-20) ÷ (-10) = + 2
L. $-20/10 = -2$
M. (-20) ÷ y = $-20/y$
N. $-20/-y = 20/y$

When multiplying negatives:
An even # of (-)'s will make a POSITIVE answer
An odd # of (-)'s will make a NEGATIVE answer

O. (- 5)(- 3)(- 2)(- 1) = + 30
P. (- 3)(- 2)(- 1) = - 6

Positive x Positive = +
Negative x Negative = +
Positive x Negative = -

<u>Same rules apply for division</u>

Multiplying & Dividing #'s & Variables

Practice:

1. -5(-8) =
See ex. G or J for reference

2. (-4) · 9 =
ex. H

3. 10 * -5 =
ex. H

4. 3 x 3 =
ex. A

5. (-1)(-3)(-2)(-2) =
ex. O

6. (-3)(-3)(-3) =
ex. P

7. -7(y) =
ex. J or I

1. $^{-10}/_{5}$ =
ex. L

2. $^{(-6)}/_{(-3)}$ =
ex. K

3. 12 ÷ 4 =
ex. D

4. -100 ÷ 10 =
ex. L

5. $^{20}/_{-2}$ =
ex. L

6. -50 ÷ -2 =
ex. K

7. -16 ÷ y =
ex. M

Written by April Chloe Terrazas

Practice ANSWERS

1. (-5)(-8), (-) x (-) = (+), 5 x 8 = 40, **answer is + 40**
2. (-4) · 9, (-) x (+) = (-), 4 x 9 = 36, **answer is - 36**
3. 10 * -5, (+) x (-) = (-), 10 x 5 = 50, **answer is - 50**
4. 3 x 3, (+) x (+) = (+), 3 x 3 = 9, **answer is + 9**
5. (-1)(-3)(-2)(-2), EVEN # of NEGATIVE SIGNS, positive, 1 x 3 x 2 x 2 = 12, **answer is + 12**
6. (-3)(-3)(-3), ODD # of NEGATIVE SIGNS, negative, 3 x 3 x 3 = 27, **answer is - 27**
7. -7 x y, (-) x (+) = (-), 7 x y= 7y, **answer is -7y**

1. $^{-10}/_{5}$, (-) ÷ (+) = (-), 10 ÷ 5 = 2, **answer is - 2**
2. $^{(-6)}/_{(-3)}$, (-) ÷ (-) = (+), 6 ÷ 3 = 2, **answer is + 2**
3. 12 ÷ 4, (+) ÷ (+) = (+), 12 ÷ 4 = 3, **answer is + 3**
4. -100 ÷ 10, (-) ÷ (+) = (-), 100 ÷ 10 = 10, **answer is -10**
5. $^{20}/_{-2}$, (+) ÷ (-) = (-), 20 ÷ 2 = 10, **answer is - 10**
6. -50 ÷ -2, (-) ÷ (-) = (+), 50 ÷ 2 = 25, **answer is + 25**
7. -16 ÷ y, (-) ÷ (+) = (-), 16 ÷ y = $^{16}/_{y}$, **answer is -16/y**

Order of Operations

Please Excuse My Dear Aunt Sally

PEMDAS

Parentheses, Exponents, Multiply, Divide, Add, Subtract

Parentheses FIRST

Exponents SECOND

(Multiply and Divide at the same time)

(Add and Subtract FROM LEFT TO RIGHT, whichever comes first)

A. $8 + 3 \times 4$

Correct way to solve:

$8 + 3 \times 4$

Multiplication comes before addition so you multiply 3 x 4 FIRST.

$8 + 12$

Now add.

Answer = 20

If you were to add 8 + 3 first, you will get the WRONG ANSWER!

$8 + 3 \times 4$

11×4

Answer = 44

INCORRECT!

The correct answer is 20.

C. $6 + 3(8 - 3)^2 - 4 \times 2$

$6 + 3(8 - 3)^2 - 4 \times 2$

$6 + 3(5)^2 - 4 \times 2$

$6 + 3(25) - 4 \times 2$

$6 + 75 - 8$

Answer = 73

PEMDAS

B. $12 - 3(5 - 1) + 2^2 + 6 \times 3$

Correct way to solve:

$12 - 3(5 - 1) + 2^2 + 6 \times 3$

Parentheses first

$12 - 3(4) + 2^2 + 6 \times 3$

Exponents next

$12 - 3(4) + 4 + 6 \times 3$

Multiplication next

$12 - 12 + 4 + 18$

Subtraction is first going *left to right* in this ex.

$0 + 4 + 18$

Finally, add.

Answer = 22

D. $12 - 18 \div 3 + (2 \times 2)^2 + 3 \times 5$

$12 - 18 \div 3 + (2 \times 2)^2 + 3 \times 5$

$12 - 18 \div 3 + (4)^2 + 3 \times 5$

$12 - 18 \div 3 + 16 + 3 \times 5$

$12 - 6 + 16 + 15$

Answer = 37

E. $40 + [\ 3(8+1)\ ]$

$40 + [\ 3(8+1)\ ]$

**Work the innermost parentheses 1st.*

$40 + [\ 3(9)\ ]$

$40 + 27$

Answer = 67

More practice: Algebra Is Easy Part 1 SUCCESS BOOK (Workbook + Test Book)

Order of Operations

Practice:

1. $9 + 6 \times 8 =$
See example A for reference

2. $9 \times 2 - 7 =$
ex. A

3. $5(4) + 2 \times 3 =$
ex. A or C

4. $4 - 3(5 \times 4) + 6^2 =$
ex. B or D

5. $18 \div 2 + 3^3 - 4(9 - 7)^2 =$
ex. B or D

6. $- 5^3 \div 5 + 6(8 - 3) =$
ex. B or D

7. $3 [7 + 4(9 + 1) - 5] =$
ex. E

Written by April Chloe Terrazas

Practice ANSWERS

1. $9 + 6 \times 8 = 57$
$9 + 6 \times 8$
$9 + 48$
$= 57$

2. $9 \times 2 - 7 = 11$
$9 \times 2 - 7$
$18 - 7$
$= 11$

3. $5(4) + 2 \times 3 = 26$
$5(4) + 2 \times 3$
$20 + 6$
$= 26$

4. $4 - 3(5 \times 4) + 6^2 = -20$
$4 - 3(5 \times 4) + 6^2$
$4 - 3 (20) + 6^2$
$4 - 3(20) + 36$
$4 - 60 + 36$
$- 56 + 36$
$= -20$

5. $18 \div 2 + 3^3 - 4(9 - 7)^2 = 20$
$18 \div 2 + 3^3 - 4(9 - 7)^2$
$18 \div 2 + 3^3 - 4(2)^2$
$18 \div 2 + 27 - 4(4)$
$9 + 27 - 16$
$= 20$

6. $- 5^3 \div 5 + 6(8 - 3) = 5$
$- 5^3 \div 5 + 6(8 - 3)$
$- 5^3 \div 5 + 6(5)$
$- 125 \div 5 + 6(5)$
$- 25 + 30$
$= 5$

7. $3 [7 + 4(9 + 1) - 5] = 126$
$3 [7 + 4(9 + 1) - 5]$
$3 [7 + 4(10) - 5]$
$3 [7 + 40 - 5]$
$3 [42]$
$= 126$

Distributive Property

The distributive property is exactly like it sounds. You are DISTRIBUTING (multiplying) some number (or variable) to other numbers and variables inside the parentheses. If there are only numbers inside the parentheses, simplify inside the parentheses FIRST, then multiply (examples A and B).

If there is a variable inside the parentheses, you cannot simplify any further. So, multiply the number (or variable) outside the parentheses times EACH number and/or variable inside the parentheses (example C, D, E).

Positive Numbers, Variables

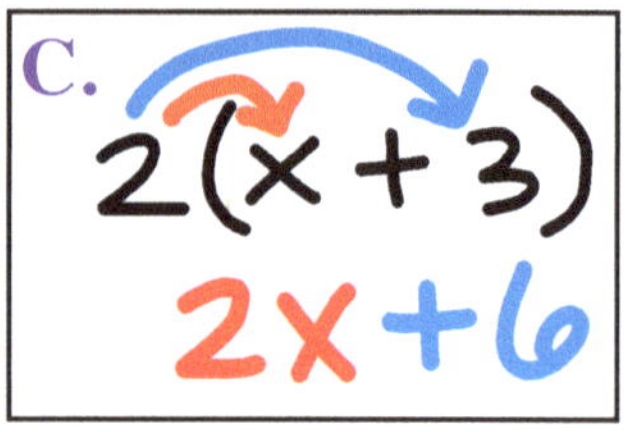

A. $3(4+2) = 3(6) = 18$

B. $4(3+7-6) = 4(10-6) = 4(4) = 16$

C. $2(x+3) = 2(x) + 2(3) = 2x + 6$

D. $x(x+y+z) = x(x) + x(y) + x(z) = x^2 + xy + xz$

(this is the final answer, it cannot be further simplified)

E. $x^2(x^3 + y^2 + z^4) = x^2(x^3) + x^2(y^2) + x^2(z^4) =$

$x^{2+3} + x^2y^2 + x^2z^4 = x^5 + x^2y^2 + x^2z^4$

How to tell if an answer is positive or negative? Review the diagram on page 8

Negative Numbers, Variables

F. $-6(3+9) = -6(12) = -72$

G. $-7(-8-3) = -7(-11) = +77$

H. $-3(x+1) = -3(x) + (-3)(1) = -3x - 3$

I. $-x(x - 2y + z) = -x(x) + x(2y) - x(z) \quad = -x^2 + 2xy - xz$

J. $-x^3(x^4 - y^5) \quad = -x^3(x^4) - x^3(-y^5) \quad = -x^{3+4} + x^3(y^5) \quad = -x^7 + x^3y^5$

Distributive Property

Practice:

1. $4(5 + 9) =$
See example A

5. $-8(-5-1) =$
ex. G

2. $6(7 + 3 + 12) =$
ex. A or B

6. $-y(2x - y - z) =$
ex. I

3. $8(x + 4) =$
ex. C

7. $-x^4(x^2 + y^2) =$
ex. I or J

4. $x(x + y) =$
ex. C or D

8. $3x^2(x^3 - 3y^4 + 2z^2) =$
ex. E or J

Written by April Chloe Terrazas

Practice ANSWERS

1. $4(5 + 9) = 56$

Order of operations, parentheses first, 5+9 = 14 *4 (14) =* ***56***

2. $6(7 + 3 + 12) = 132$

Order of ops, P first, 7 + 3 + 12 =22 *6 (22) =* ***132***

3. $8(x + 4) = 8x + 32$

Cannot simplify further inside parentheses so DISTRIBUTE the 8 to both the x and the 4, 8 times x is 8x, 8 times 4 is 32, ***8x + 32***

4. $x(x + y) = x^2 + xy$

Cannot simplify further inside parentheses so DISTRIBUTE the x to both the x and y, x times x is x^2, x times y is xy, ***$x^2 + xy$***

5. $-8(-5-1) = +48$

Order of ops, P first, -5 - 1 = -6 *-8 (-6) =* ***+ 48*** *negative x negative = positive*

6. $-y(2x - y - z) = -2xy + y^2 + yz$

Cannot simplify further inside parentheses so DISTRIBUTE the -y to the 2x, -y and -z,

-y times 2x is -2xy, -y times -y is + y^2, -y times -z is + yz. ***$-2xy + y^2 + yz$***

7. $-x^4(x^2 + y^2) = -x^6 - x^4y^2$

Distribute $-x^4$ to x^2 and y^2, $-x^4$ times x^2 is $-x^6$ (add the exponents), $-x^4$ times y^2 is $-x^4y^2$, ***$-x^6 - x^4y^2$***

8. $3x^2(x^3 - 3y^4 + 2z^2) = 3x^5 - 9x^2y^4 + 6x^2z^2$

Distribute $3x^2$ to x^3, $-3y^4$ and $2z^2$, $3x^2$ times x^3 is $3x^5$ (add exponents), $3x^2$ times $-3y^4$ is $-9x^2y^4$, $3x^2$ times $2z^2$ is $6x^2z^2$

$3x^5 - 9x^2y^4 + 6x^2z^2$

Evaluating Algebraic Expressions

To "EVALUATE AN EXPRESSION," you are plugging in a given value for a given variable (letter) and solving for a number.

Always use (PARENTHESES) when you "plug in" the value for the variable.

A. Evaluate the expression x + 2y when x = 3 and y = 1

First, plug in the numbers to their specific variable (letter) using parentheses.

x + 2 y

(3) + 2(1), then solve, 3 + 2 = **5**

B. Evaluate the expression 5 (3x - 4y) when x = - 1 and y = - 7

First, plug in the numbers to their specific variable (letter) using parentheses.

5 [**3**(-1) - **4**(-7)], order of operations-do inside parentheses first

5 (-3 + 28), minus 4 and negative 7 will make positive 28 when multiplied

5 (25) = **125**

C. Evaluate the expression x^2 + (y^3 - 5) when x = 3 and y = - 3

$(3)^2$ + [$(- 3)^3$ - **5**], order of operations-do exponents first.

9 + [-27 - 5], negative 3 to the third power = (-3)(-3)(-3) = - 27

9 + [-32], now that parentheses have been simplified, add

9 + -32 = **- 23** **different signs subtract**

Evaluate the following problems when x = 2, y = - 5, z = - 1

1. $2x + y =$

2. $3 (5x + z) =$

3. $- 4 (x + 3y - 2z) =$

4. $y^3 + 2x =$

5. $z^3 + (4x^2 + 9) =$

6. $9x - 5y + 3z =$

7. $2x^5 (12 - 2y) =$

8. $x + y + z =$

1.	2(2) + (-5)	= 4 + (-5)	= -1		
2.	3 [5(2) + (-1)]	= 3 [10 + -1]	= 3 [9]	= 27	
3.	-4 [(2) + 3(-5) - 2(-1)]	= -4 [2 - 15 + 2]	= -4 [-11]	= 44	
4.	$(-5)^3$ + 2 (2)	= -125 + 4	= -121		
5.	(-1) 3 + [$4(2)^2$ + 9]	= -1 + [4(4) + 9]	= -1 + [16 + 9]	= -1 + 25	= 24
6.	9(2) - 5(-5) + 3(-1)	= 18 + 25 - 3	= 40		
7.	$2(2)^5$ [12 - 2(-5)]	= 2(32) [12 + 10]	= 64 [22]	= 1408	
8.	(2) + (-5) + (-1)	= 2 - 5 - 1	= -4		

More practice: Algebra Is Easy Part 1 SUCCESS BOOK (Workbook + Test Book)

Absolute Value

Absolute value is **the distance a value is from 0**. No matter the sign, the absolute value is ALWAYS positive.
The absolute value of -3 is 3 because -3 is 3 units from 0. The absolute value of +3 is 3 because +3 is 3 units from 0.

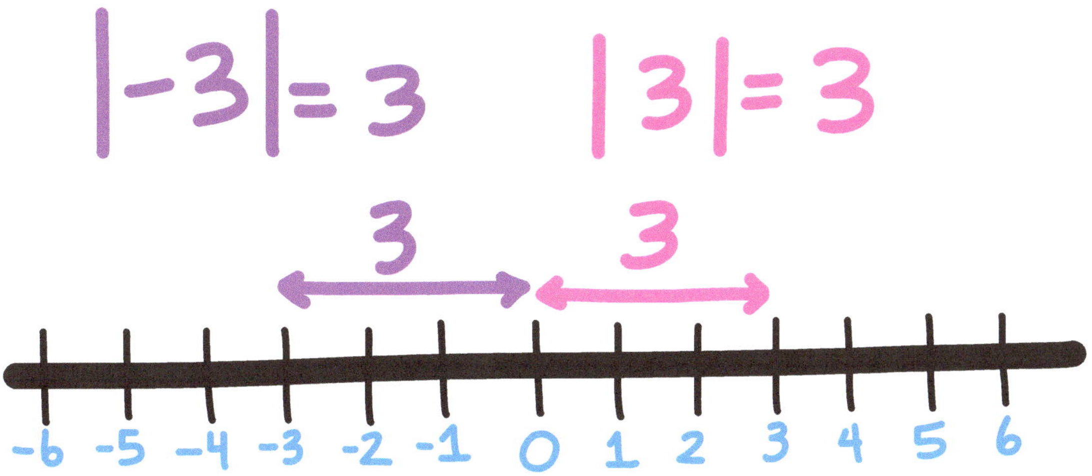

A. | -2 | = **2**

-2 is 2 units from 0.
Absolute value = +2

B. - | -2 | = **- 2**

-2 is 2 units from 0.
Absolute value = +2
Negative sign remains
and is multiplied by +2 = - 2

C. | 8 | = **8**

8 is 8 units from 0.
Absolute value = +8

D. - | 8 | = **- 8**

8 is 8 units from 0.
Absolute value = +8
Negative sign remains
and is multiplied by +8 = - 8

E. | 4 + 12 | = **16**
4 + 12 = 16
16 is 16 units from 0.
Absolute value = +16

F. - | - 5 - 2 | = **- 7**
- 5 - 2 = - 7
- 7 is 7 units from 0.
Absolute value = +7
Negative sign remains
and is multiplied by +7 = - 7

G. | 20 - 30 | = **10**
20 - 30 = - 10
-10 is 10 units from 0.
Absolute value = +10

H. - | 20 - 30 | = **- 10**
20 - 30 = - 10
-10 is 10 units from 0.
Absolute value = +10
Negative sign remains
and is multiplied by +10 = - 10

Practice:

1. | -1 | =
2. | -18 | =
3. - | 5 + 5 | =
4. | -25 | =
5. - | - 9 - 3 | =
6. | 7 - 15 | =
7. - | 7 - 15 | =
8. | 250 - 25 | =

Practice Answers:
1. 1 2. 18 3. - 10 4. 25 5. - 12 6. 8 7. - 8 8. 225

Written by April Chloe Terrazas

Adding & Subtracting Variables

Adding and subtracting variables is similar to adding and subtracting numbers.

First, look for "LIKE TERMS" that you can combine.

For example, 3x and 8x are LIKE TERMS because they are both x's to the first power. (x^1)

In a real life situation you can use this example:

If I have 3 apples and you have 8 apples, how many apples do we have all together?

This is $\mathbf{3x + 8x = 11x}$*, or 11 apples.*

Or, If you have 8 apples and I have 3 apples, how many more apples do you have than me?

This is $\mathbf{8x - 3x = 5x}$*, or 5 more apples.*

YOU CAN ONLY ADD AND SUBTRACT LIKE TERMS!

Once you have identified the LIKE TERMS, it is like a simple addition or subtraction problem.

Like terms always have the same exponent.

Examples of LIKE TERMS:	Adding/Subtracting LIKE TERMS:
$-5x, x, 2x, 3x, 10x, 25x$	$x + 2x + 3x = \mathbf{6x}$
$-3xy, 8xy, 100xy, 525xy$	$8xy + 100xy = \mathbf{108xy}$
$-2abc, 9abc, 15abc$	$-2abc + 9abc + 15abc = \mathbf{22abc}$
$-4x^2, -2x^2, x^2, 11x^2, 25x^2$	$-4x^2 - 2x^2 + 11x^2 = \mathbf{5x^2}$
$3x^2y, 6x^2y, 10x^2y$	$3x^2y + 6x^2y + 10x^2y = \mathbf{19x^2y}$

Examples of *UNLIKE* TERMS:	Adding/Subtracting UNLIKE TERMS:
$8x, 5y, 6z$	$8x + 5y + 6z = \mathbf{8x + 5y + 6z}$
$9, 9x, 9x^2, 9x^3$	$9 - 9x^2 = \mathbf{9 - 9x^2}$
$3a, 3ab, 3abc$	$3a + 3ab + 3abc = \mathbf{3a + 3ab + 3abc}$
$2, 18y, 21z$	$2 - 18y = \mathbf{2 - 18y}$

UNlike terms CANNOT be added or subtracted!

When adding or subtracting UNlike terms, the answer is simply RE-writing the terms being added or subtracted. It cannot be simplified any further.

More examples of adding/subtracting LIKE terms:

A. $x + 5x = \mathbf{6x}$ — $1 + 5 = \mathbf{6}$

B. $10y - 3y = \mathbf{7y}$ — $10 - 3 = \mathbf{7}$

C. $2x + 3x + 7y + y = \mathbf{5x + 8y}$ — $2 + 3 = \mathbf{5}$, $7 + 1 = \mathbf{8}$

D. $3x^2 - x^2 + 10ab + 2ab = \mathbf{2x^2 + 12ab}$ — $3 - 1 = \mathbf{2}$, $10 + 2 = \mathbf{12}$

E. $9xy - 12xy = \mathbf{-3xy}$ — $9 - 12 = \mathbf{-3}$

F. $4a^3 - 3a^3 + 7b^2 - 16b^2 = \mathbf{a^3 - 9b^2}$ — $4 - 3 = \mathbf{1}$, $7 - 16 = \mathbf{-9}$

Adding & Subtracting Variables

Practice:

1. $x + 3x =$

2. $2abc - 10abc =$

3. $18x + 21x =$

4. $x^2 + 5x^2 - 13x^2 =$

5. $-5a + 12a + 2a =$

6. $12xy - 10xy =$

7. $9x^3 + 5x^3 =$

8. $6b + 12b - 2b =$

9. $11y^3 + 5y^3 =$

10. $20z - z =$

11. $18x + 12y =$

12. $2x + 4x + 7y - 3y =$

13. $7abc + 12xyz =$

14. $3a^2 + 4b^3 + a^2 - 2b^3 =$

15. $12 - 21b =$

16. $2x^2y + 5x^2y =$

Written by April Chloe Terrazas

Practice Answers:

1.	$1x + 3x =$ **$4x$**	$1 + 3 = 4$	9.	$11y^3 + 5y^3 =$ **$16y^3$**	$11 + 5 = 16$
2.	$2abc - 10abc =$ **$-8abc$**	$2 - 10 = -8$	10.	$20z - z =$ **$19z$**	$20 - 1 = 19$
3.	$18x + 21x =$ **$39x$**	$18 + 21 = 39$	11.	$18x + 12y =$ **$18x + 12y$**	UNLIKE
4.	$1x^2 + 5x^2 - 13x^2 =$ **$-7x^2$**	$1 + 5 - 13 = -7$	12.	$2x + 4x + 7y - 3y =$ **$6x + 4y$**	$2+4 = 6, 7-3 = 4$
5.	$-5a + 12a + 2a =$ **$9a$**	$-5 + 12 + 2 = 9$	13.	$7abc + 12xyz =$ **$7abc + 12xyz$**	UNLIKE
6.	$12xy - 10xy =$ **$2xy$**	$12 - 10 = 2$	14.	$3a^2 + a^2 + 4b^3 - 2b^3 =$ **$4a^2 + 2b^3$**	
7.	$9x^3 + 5x^3 =$ **$14x^3$**	$9 + 5 = 14$	15.	$12 - 21b =$ **$12 - 21b$**	UNLIKE
8.	$6b + 12b - 2b =$ **$16b$**	$6 + 12 - 2 = 16$	16.	$2x^2y + 5x^2y =$ **$7x^2y$**	$2 + 5 = 7$

Multiplying & Dividing Variables

Different variables (unlike terms) can be multiplied and divided

When multiplying a number times a variable (letter), simply write the number next to the variable and multiplication is implied by the number and letter being side by side.

For example:

$3(y) = 3y$

$8 \text{ times } x = 8x$

$12 \cdot abc = 12abc$

Multiplying variables, ADD the exponent

BUT, only add on the SAME base

$x \cdot x \cdot x = x^{1+1+1} = \mathbf{x^3}$

$y^2 \cdot y^4 \cdot y^5 = y^{2+4+5} = \mathbf{y^{11}}$

$\mathbf{3a^2} \cdot \mathbf{5a} \cdot \mathbf{6b^2} = 3 \cdot 5\, a^{2+1} \cdot 6b^2 = \mathbf{90a^3b^2}$

$6x \cdot 8x = 48x^2$

$4y^2 \cdot 2y^3 = 8y^5$

When dividing a number and a variable (letter), simply write the number over or under the variable and division is implied by the number and letter making a fraction.

For example:

$3 \div x = 3/x$

$x \text{ divided by } 12 = x/12$

$y \div 7 = y/7$

Dividing variables, SUBTRACT the NUMERATOR exponent minus the DENOMINATOR exponent.

BUT, only subtract on the same base

$$\frac{a^4}{a^2} = \frac{a \cdot a \cdot a \cdot a}{a \cdot a} = a^{4-2} = \mathbf{a^2}$$

$$\frac{x^{10}}{x^5} = x^{10-5} = x^5$$

More examples multiplying:

Multiply the whole numbers in front (coefficent) separate from the variable(s).

A. $9x \cdot 2x \cdot x = 9 \cdot 2 \cdot x^{1+1+1} = \mathbf{18x^3}$

B. $2a^2(5a) = 2 \cdot 5 \cdot a^{2+1} = \mathbf{10a^3}$

C. $3ab \cdot 6a \cdot 2b = 3 \cdot 6 \cdot 2 \cdot a^{1+1} \cdot b^{1+1} = \mathbf{36a^2b^2}$

D. $4x^3 \cdot 2x^2 \cdot x^4 = 4 \cdot 2 \cdot x^{3+2+4} = \mathbf{8x^9}$

E. $2x^5y^7 \cdot 3x^3y^8 = 2 \cdot 3 \cdot x^{5+3} \cdot y^{7+8} = \mathbf{6x^8y^{15}}$

F. $3a^2(4a^2b^3) = 3 \cdot 4 \cdot a^{2+2} \cdot b^3 = \mathbf{12a^4b^3}$

G. $7x(x^4 + x^5y^2) = 7 \cdot x^{1+4} + 7 \cdot x^{1+5}y^2$

**distributive property* $= \mathbf{7x^5 + 7x^6y^2}$

H. $2y^2(x^2y^2 - 3y^4) = 2 \cdot x^2 \cdot y^{2+2} - 2 \cdot 3 \cdot y^{2+4}$

**distributive property* $= \mathbf{2x^2y^4 - 6y^6}$

More examples dividing:

Divide the whole numbers in front of the variables separate from the variables.

I. $\dfrac{12x^7}{6x^3} = 12/6\; x^{7-3} = \mathbf{2x^4}$

J. $\dfrac{3a^9}{4a^2} = 3/4\; a^{9-2} = \dfrac{\mathbf{3a^7}}{\mathbf{4}}$

K. $\dfrac{20x^2y^9}{5x^2y^6} = 20/5\; x^{2-2}\, y^{9-6} = 4x^0y^3 = \mathbf{4y^3}$

L. $\dfrac{18a^5b^{11}c^4}{10a^2b^5c^6} = 18/10\; a^{5-2}\, b^{11-5}\, c^{4-6} = \dfrac{\mathbf{9a^3b^6c^{-2}}}{\mathbf{5}}$

NEGATIVE EXPONENT!

Your final answer cannot contain a negative exponent. To change a negative exponent to postive, simply move it from its current position in the numerator (or denominator) to the oppositive positition, the denominator (or numerator). In example L, the negative exponent is in the NUMERATOR, so we will move it DOWN TO THE DENOMINATOR in order to make it positive.

$$\frac{\mathbf{9a^3b^6c^{-2}}}{\mathbf{5}} = \frac{\mathbf{9a^3b^6}}{\mathbf{5c^2}}$$

This is the final answer with all positive exponents

More practice: Algebra Is Easy Part 1 SUCCESS BOOK (Workbook + Test Book)

Multiplying & Dividing Variables

Practice:

1. $5(x) =$
2. $10 \cdot zyx =$
3. $2a^2 \cdot 3a^3 =$
4. $10x(4x^2 + 3x^3) =$
5. $4a^4 \cdot 6a^{10} \cdot 2a^8 =$
6. $3y^3(4x^2y^2 - 2x^3y^4) =$
7. $12 \div 2y =$
8. $\dfrac{6a^{12}}{8a^4} =$
9. $\dfrac{120x^7y^2}{6x^3y} =$
10. $\dfrac{20a^7b^4}{4a^4b^2} =$
11. $\dfrac{64x^7y^5z^3}{8x^3y^3z^3} =$
12. $\dfrac{26a^7b^8c^{12}}{4a^{10}b^3c^{15}} =$

Practice Answers:

1. $5(x) = 5x$
2. $10 \cdot xyz = 10xyz$
3. $2 \cdot 3 \cdot a^{2+3} = 6a^5$
4. $10 \cdot 4 \cdot x^{1+2} + 10 \cdot 3 \cdot x^{1+3} = 40x^3 + 30x^4$
5. $4 \cdot 6 \cdot 2 \cdot a^{4+10+8} = 48a^{22}$
6. $3 \cdot 4 \cdot x^2 \cdot y^{3+2} - 3 \cdot 2 \cdot x^3 \cdot y^{3+4} = 12x^2y^5 - 6x^3y^7$
7. $12 \div 2y = {}^{12}\!/_{2y} = {}^{6}\!/_{y}$
8. ${}^{6}\!/_{8} \cdot a^{12-4} = {}^{3a^8}\!/_{4}$
9. ${}^{120}\!/_{6} \cdot x^{7-3} \cdot y^{2-1} = 20x^4y^1 = 20x^4y$
10. ${}^{20}\!/_{4} \cdot a^{7-4}b^{4-2} = 5a^3b^2$
11. ${}^{64}\!/_{8} \cdot x^{7-3}y^{5-3}z^{3-3} = 8x^4y^2z^0 = 8x^4y^2$
12. ${}^{26}\!/_{4} \cdot a^{7-10}b^{8-3}c^{12-15} = \dfrac{13a^{-3}b^5c^{-3}}{2} = \dfrac{13b^5}{2a^3c^3}$

Keep going

YOU'RE

DOING

GREAT!

Written by April Chloe Terrazas

Fractions: Simplifying

A fraction is a DIVISION PROBLEM. Simple.

Types of Fractions:

A **PROPER fraction** has a SMALLER NUMERATOR than denominator
For example:

$\frac{1}{2}$

$\frac{3}{4}$

$\frac{7}{10}$

$\frac{115}{211}$

An **IMPROPER fraction** has a LARGER NUMERATOR than denominator
For example:

$\frac{12}{5}$

$\frac{16}{11}$

$\frac{7}{4}$

$\frac{125}{100}$

A **MIXED NUMBER** is a whole number combined with a fraction
For example:

$8\frac{1}{5}$

$4\frac{3}{4}$

$3\frac{7}{10}$

$12\ \frac{125}{500}$

A fraction is **SIMPLIFIED** when there does not exist another number that can be divided into the numerator AND the denominator evenly. It cannot be further REDUCED. **(Reducing happens by dividing)**

The following are SIMPLIFED FRACTIONS:

$\frac{1}{4}$ $\frac{1}{3}$ $\frac{1}{2}$ $\frac{2}{3}$ $\frac{4}{5}$ $\frac{9}{10}$ $\frac{11}{12}$

A fraction is **NOT simplified** when the numerator and denominator can still be divided by a number evenly. All of the fractions below can be further REDUCED, or SIMPLIFIED.

The following are UNSIMPLIFED FRACTIONS:

$\frac{10}{40}$ $\frac{2}{6}$ $\frac{2}{4}$ $\frac{8}{12}$ $\frac{12}{20}$ $\frac{18}{20}$ $\frac{100}{120}$

HOW TO SIMPLIFY FRACTIONS

Find a number that can be divided evenly into BOTH the numerator AND denominator, and divide.

A. $\frac{10}{20} = \frac{10 \div 10}{20 \div 10} = \frac{1}{2}$ Both the numerator and denominator are *divisible by 10*

B. $\frac{15}{20} = \frac{15 \div 5}{20 \div 5} = \frac{3}{4}$ Both the numerator and denominator are *divisible by 5*

C. $\frac{6}{8} = \frac{6 \div 2}{8 \div 2} = \frac{3}{4}$ Both the numerator and denominator are *divisible by 2*

D. $\frac{3}{12} = \frac{3 \div 3}{12 \div 3} = \frac{1}{4}$ Both the numerator and denominator are *divisible by 3*

All of these fractions are reduced, or simplified. They cannot be divided by another number in the numerator and denominator evenly.

Practice - Simplify the following fractions:

1. $\frac{15}{40} =$

2. $\frac{4}{12} =$

3. $\frac{18}{20} =$

4. $\frac{6}{10} =$

5. $\frac{7}{21} =$

6. $\frac{15}{60} =$

Practice Answers:

1. divide by 5, $\frac{3}{8}$

2. divide by 4, $\frac{1}{3}$

3. divide by 2, $\frac{9}{10}$

4. divide by 2, $\frac{3}{5}$

5. divide by 7, $\frac{1}{3}$

6. divide by 15, $\frac{1}{4}$

Fractions: Improper vs. Mixed

Converting between Mixed Numbers and Improper Fractions

Mixed Number to Improper Fraction

Multiply the denominator times the whole number, then add the numerator.

In this example, multiply the denominator (4) times the whole number (2) then add the numerator (3).

$$4 \times 2 + 3 = 11$$

Then write that number over the existing denominator (4).

$$2\frac{3}{4} = \frac{11}{4}$$

Improper Fraction to Mixed Number

Remember, a fraction is a division problem.
Divide the numerator by the denominator to get the WHOLE NUMBER, then use the remainder as the numerator of the fraction.

In this example, how many times does the denominator (4) go into the numerator (11)? __2 times__

2 is the whole number part of the mixed number.

11 ÷ 4 = 2 remainder (r.) 3

The remainder becomes the numerator.

$$\frac{11}{4} = 2\frac{3}{4}$$

In both cases, **THE DENOMINATOR STAYS THE SAME**

Whether converting from Mixed Number to Improper Fraction, or Improper Fraction to Mixed Number
the denominator remains the same.

Convert from Mixed # to Improper Fraction:

A. $1\frac{4}{5} = \frac{5 \times 1 + 4}{5} = \frac{5 + 4}{5} = \frac{9}{5}$

B. $7\frac{3}{8} = \frac{8 \times 7 + 3}{8} = \frac{56 + 3}{8} = \frac{59}{8}$

C. $5\frac{2}{9} = \frac{9 \times 5 + 2}{9} = \frac{45 + 2}{9} = \frac{47}{9}$

Convert from Improper Fraction to Mixed #:

D. $\frac{10}{3} = 10 \div 3 = 3 \text{ r. } 1 = 3\frac{1}{3}$

E. $\frac{25}{4} = 25 \div 4 = 6 \text{ r. } 1 = 6\frac{1}{4}$

F. $\frac{42}{6} = 42 \div 6 = 7 \text{ r. } 0 = 7\frac{0}{3} = 7$

Practice Problems: Convert the Mixed Numbers to Improper Fractions and the Improper Fractions to Mixed Numbers

1. $2\frac{3}{5} =$

2. $5\frac{9}{10} =$

3. $3\frac{1}{6} =$

4. $9\frac{7}{9} =$

4. $\frac{12}{7} =$

5. $\frac{35}{3} =$

6. $\frac{46}{5} =$

7. $\frac{18}{4} =$

1) 5x2+3 = 13/5 2) 10x5+9 = 59/10 3) 6x3+1 = 19/6 4) 9x9+7 = 88/9 4) 12 ÷ 7 = 1 r. 5, 1 5/7 2) 35 ÷ 3 = 11 r. 2, 11 2/3 3) 46 ÷ 5 = 9 r. 1, 9 1/5 4) 18 ÷ 4 = 4 r. 2, 4 2/4, simplify, 4 1/2

Written by April Chloe Terrazas

Fractions: Multiplying

Multiplying fractions is EASY, FOLKS!!!

Multiply the numerator x numerator and denominator x denominator.

Then simplify the answer.

A. $\frac{1}{2} \times \frac{3}{4} = \frac{1 \times 3}{2 \times 4} = \frac{3}{8}$

$3/8$ is already in simplest form. Done.

B. $\frac{4}{5} \times \frac{3}{8} = \frac{4 \times 3}{5 \times 8} = \frac{12}{40} = \frac{12 \div 4}{40 \div 4} = \frac{3}{10}$

$12/40$ can be simplified by dividing the numerator and denominator by 4 to get $3/10$ for the final answer.

C. $1\frac{4}{5} \times \frac{1}{3} = \frac{9}{5} \times \frac{1}{3} = \frac{9}{15} = \frac{9 \div 3}{15 \div 3} = \frac{3}{5}$

First, convert $1\,4/5$ to an IMPROPER FRACTION, then multiply.

$1\frac{4}{5} = \frac{5 \times 1 + 4}{5} = \frac{5 + 4}{5} = \frac{9}{5}$

Tip: Reduce BEFORE multiplying to get to the answer faster! The 9 and the 3 can REDUCE to 3 and 1. More details in FULL BOOK WEBINAR.

$\frac{\not{9}}{5} \times \frac{1}{\not{3}} = \frac{3}{5} \times \frac{1}{1} = \frac{3}{5}$

Practice:

1. $\frac{1}{6} \times \frac{3}{7} =$

2. $\frac{5}{9} \times \frac{2}{15} =$

3. $\frac{4}{5} \times \frac{10}{12} =$

4. $\frac{1}{8} \times \frac{3}{5} =$

5. $2\frac{3}{5} \times \frac{4}{9} =$

6. $1\frac{1}{4} \times \frac{2}{3} =$

7. $5\frac{2}{7} \times \frac{1}{8} =$

8. $8\frac{4}{7} \times 3\frac{1}{6} =$

Practice Answers:

1. $1/6 \times 3/7$, *reduce the 6 and 3 to 2 and 1* $= 1/2 \times 1/7 = 1/14$

2. $5/9 \times 2/15$, *reduce the 5 and 15 to 1 and 3* $= 1/9 \times 2/3 = 2/27$

3. $4/5 \times 10/12$, *reduce the 5 and 10 to 1 and 2 and reduce the 4 and 12 to 1 and 3* $= 1/1 \times 2/3 = 2/3$

4. $1/8 \times 3/5$, *nothing can be reduced, multiply* $= 3/40$

5. $2\,3/5 = 13/5 \times 4/9$, *cannot be reduced, multiply* $= 52/45 = 1\,7/45$

6. $1\,1/4 = 5/4 \times 2/3$, *reduce the 4 and 2 to 2 and 1* $= 5/2 \times 1/3 = 5/6$

7. $5\,2/7 = 37/7 \times 1/8$, *cannot be reduced, multiply* $= 37/56$

8. $8\,4/7 = 60/7$, $3\,1/6 = 19/6$, *reduce the 60 and 6 to 10 and 1* $= 10/7 \times 19/1 = 190/7 = 27\,1/7$

Fractions: Dividing

Dividing fractions is EASY, FOLKS!!!

First, flip the <u>second fraction</u>, then multiply.

Multiply the **numerator x numerator** and **denominator x denominator**.

Then **simplify the answer**.

$$\boxed{\frac{1}{2} \div \frac{3}{4}} = \boxed{\frac{1}{2} \times \frac{4}{3}} = \frac{4}{6} = \frac{4 \div 2}{6 \div 2} = \frac{2}{3}$$

or REDUCE, then multiply

$$\boxed{\frac{1}{2} \div \frac{3}{4}} = \boxed{\frac{1}{\cancel{2}} \times \frac{\cancel{4}}{3}} = \frac{1}{1} \times \frac{2}{3} = \frac{2}{3}$$

Dividing fractions is simply multiplying by the reciprocal (flip) of the second fraction!

Mixed Number? Convert to IMPROPER FRACTION, then flip the second fraction and multiply!

$$\boxed{1\frac{4}{5} \div \frac{1}{3}} = \frac{9}{5} \times \frac{3}{1} = \frac{27}{5} = 5\frac{2}{5}$$

Practice:

1. $\frac{1}{6} \div \frac{3}{7} =$
2. $\frac{5}{9} \div \frac{2}{15} =$
3. $\frac{4}{5} \div \frac{10}{11} =$
4. $\frac{1}{8} \div \frac{3}{5} =$
5. $2\frac{3}{5} \div \frac{4}{9} =$
6. $1\frac{1}{4} \div \frac{2}{3} =$
7. $5\frac{2}{7} \div \frac{1}{8} =$
8. $8\frac{4}{7} \div 3\frac{1}{6} =$

Practice Answers:

1. $1/6 \times 7/3 = 7/18$
2. $5/9 \times 15/2 = 75/18$, *divide by 3* $= 25/6 = 4\ 1/6$
3. $4/5 \times 11/10$, *reduce 4 and 10 to 2 and 5* $= 2/5 \times 11/5 = 22/25$
4. $1/8 \times 5/3$, *nothing can be reduced, multiply* $= 5/24$
5. $2\,3/5 = 13/5 \times 9/4$, *cannot be reduced, multiply* $= 117/20 = 5\ 17/20$
6. $1\,1/4 = 5/4 \times 3/2$, *cannot be reduced, multiply* $= 15/8 = 1\,7/8$
7. $5\,2/7 = 37/7 \times 8/1$, *cannot be reduced, multiply* $= 296/7 = 42\,2/7$
8. $8\,4/7 = 60/7$, $3\,1/6 = 19/6$ IIIII $60/7 \times 6/19 = 360/133 = 2\ 94/133$

Algebra

is

Easy

and

YOU

CAN

DO IT!

Written by April Chloe Terrazas

Exponents: Intro

An exponent tells you how many times to multiply a number TIMES ITSELF.

$2^3 = 2 \times 2 \times 2 = 8$

$5^2 = 5 \times 5 = 25$

$3^5 = 3 \times 3 \times 3 \times 3 \times 3 = 243$

$10^4 = 10 \times 10 \times 10 \times 10 = 10{,}000$

$3^2 6^2 = 3 \times 3 \times 6 \times 6 = 324$

$(5 \times 2)^3 = (10)^3 = 10 \times 10 \times 10 = 1{,}000$

$75 - 3^2 = 75 - 3 \times 3 = 75 - 9 = 66$

$75 - (-3)^2 = 75 - (-3)(-3) = 75 - 9 = 66$

$75 + (-3)^2 = 75 + (-3)(-3) = 75 + 9 = 84$

$(-4)^2 = (-4) \times (-4) = 16$

$(-3)^3 = (-3) \times (-3) \times (-3) = -27$

$(-1)^5 = (-1) \cdot (-1) \cdot (-1) \cdot (-1) \cdot (-1) = -1$

$(-2)^2 = (-2) \cdot (-2) = 4$

Scientific Notation

Some numbers are VERY BIG or VERY SMALL,
for example: 45,230,000,000 or 0.00000000089
Scientific notation simplifies writing these type of numbers.
Large #'s (greater than 1) have a POSITIVE exponent on the 10.
Small #'s (less than 1) have a NEGATIVE exponent on the 10.

$x^2 = x \cdot x = x^2$

$(-y)^3 = (-y)(-y)(-y) = -y^3$

$a^4 = a \times a \times a \times a = a^4$

$(-b)^2 = (-b) \cdot (-b) = b^2$

The exponent on the "10" is found by counting the number of times the decimal must move so that there is only **ONE DIGIT** before the decimal place. (**4**.5)

A. 4,500,000 = 4.5 x 10^6

B. 689,000 = 6.89 x 10^5

C. 23,000,000,000 = 2.3 x 10^{10}

D. 721,490,000 = 7.2149 x 10^8

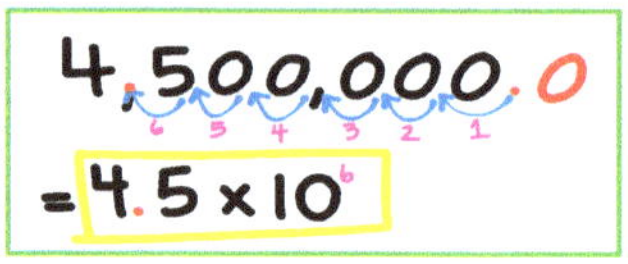

Examples A - D are large #'s with positive exponents.

Examples E - H are small #'s with negative exponents.

$-(3)^3 = -(3)(3)(3) = -27$

the negative is NOT being raised to an exponent so it just hangs out until the end, then put it in front of the answer.

$-(-5)^3 = -(-5 \cdot -5 \cdot -5) = -(-25) = +25$

calculate -5 x -5 x -5 = -25, the negative in front is still there!

What about VERY SMALL numbers?

E. 0.000423 = 4.23 x 10^{-4}

F. 0.001234 = 1.234 x 10^{-3}

G. 0.875 = 8.75 x 10^{-1}

H. 0.000091537 = 9.1537 x 10^{-5}

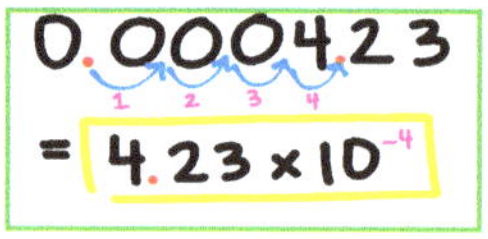

Practice

1. $3^3 =$
2. $4^2 =$
3. $(-5)^3 =$
4. $(-6)^2 =$
5. $x^4 =$
6. $(-a)^2 =$
7. $-(-4)^3 =$
8. $-(2)^2 =$
9. $5^2 2^3 =$
10. $(3 \times 6)^2 =$
11. $18 - 4^2 =$
12. $18 - (-4)^2 =$
13. $18 + (-4)^2 =$

Write in Scientific Notation

14. 2,948,000,000 =
15. 45,000 =
16. 0.002761 =
17. 0.0102 =

*Practice Answers: 1. 3x3x3 = **27** 2. 4x4 = **16** 3. (- 5)(- 5)(- 5) = **-125** 4. (- 6)(- 6) = **+36** 5. x · x · x · x = **x^4** 6. (- a)(- a) = **+ a^2** 7. - (- 4)(- 4)(- 4) = - (- 64) = **+ 64** 8. - (2)(2) = **- 4** 9. 5x5x2x2x2 = 25 x 8 = **200** 10. $(18)^2$ = **324** 11. 18 - 4 x 4 = 18 - 16 = **2** 12. 18 - (- 4)(- 4) = 18 - (+16) = 18 - 16 = **2** 13. 18 + (- 4)(- 4) = 18 + (+ 16) = 18 + 16 = **34** 14. 2.948 x 10^9 15. 4.5 x 10^4 16. 2.761 x 10^{-3} 17. 1.02 x 10^{-2}*

Exponents: Basic Uses

A. Multiplying numbers/variables w/exponents

ADD EXPONENTS, as long as the base is the same.

$$2^3 \cdot 2^2 = (2 \cdot 2 \cdot 2) \times (2 \cdot 2) = 2^{3+2} = \mathbf{2^5}$$

B. Dividing numbers/variables w/exponents

SUBTRACT EXPONENTS, as long as the base is the same.

$$\frac{a^4}{a^2} = \frac{a \cdot a \cdot a \cdot a}{a \cdot a} = a^{4-2} = \mathbf{a^2}$$

C. Exponents RAISED TO AN EXPONENT

MULTIPLY THE EXPONENTS

$$(5^2)^3 = 5^{2 \cdot 3} = \mathbf{5^6}$$

$$(x^4)^5 = x^{4 \cdot 5} = \mathbf{x^{20}}$$

$$(3^5)^{-2} = 3^{5(-2)} = \mathbf{3^{-10}}$$

D. Number/variable combos raised to an exponent

DISTRIBUTE the exponent to EVERYTHING INSIDE PARENTHESES

$$(3x)^2 = 3^2 \cdot x^2 = 9x^2$$

$$(5a^2)^3 = 5^3 \cdot a^{2 \times 3} = 125a^6$$

$$(x^2y^3)^4 = x^{2 \times 4} \cdot y^{3 \times 4} = x^8 y^{12}$$

$$\left(\frac{a^4}{a^2}\right)^3 = \frac{a^{4 \times 3}}{a^{2 \times 3}} = \frac{a^{12}}{a^6} = a^{12} - a^6 = \mathbf{a^6}$$

E. Negative exponents

Move the [number or variable] with the negative exponent from numerator to denominator, or denominator to numerator to make it become positive.

$$\frac{a^{-4}}{a^2} = \frac{1}{a^2 a^4} = \frac{1}{a^{2+4}} = \frac{1}{a^6}$$

$$\frac{a^4}{a^{-2}} = \frac{a^4 a^2}{1} = \frac{a^{4+2}}{1} = \frac{a^6}{1}$$

F. More Negative Exponents

$$x^{-1} = \frac{1}{x^1}$$

$$3b^{-3} = \frac{3}{b^3}$$

$$(2y)^{-2} = \frac{1}{2^2y^2} = \frac{1}{4y^2}$$

$$\left(\frac{y^3}{x^2}\right)^{-2} = \frac{y^{3 \times -2}}{x^{2 \times -2}} = \frac{y^{-6}}{x^{-4}} = \frac{x^4}{y^6}$$

Practice

1. $4^2 \cdot 4^3 =$
2. $\frac{x^5}{x^3} =$
3. $8^3 \cdot 8^{-5} =$
4. $(2y^2)^3 =$
5. $\frac{c^5}{c^{-3}} =$
6. $(5a^3)^3 =$
7. $4x^2 \cdot 4x^5 =$
8. $(2x)^{-3} =$
9. $(2a \cdot 3b \cdot 5c)^2 =$
10. $\left(\frac{2x^5}{3y^2}\right)^{-2} =$
11. $(x^4y^5z^8)^3 =$
12. $\left(\frac{x^{-3}}{3y^4}\right)^{-1} =$

Practice Answers: 1. $4^{2+3} = 4^5 = \mathbf{1024}$ 2. $x^{5-3} = \mathbf{x^2}$ 3. $8^{3+(-5)} = 8^{-2} = 1/8^2 = \mathbf{1/64}$ 4. $2^3 \cdot y^{2 \times 3} = \mathbf{8y^6}$ 5. $c^{5-(-3)} = c^{5+3} = \mathbf{c^8}$
6. $5^3 \cdot a^{3 \times 3} = \mathbf{125a^9}$ 7. $4 \cdot 4 \cdot x^{2+5} = \mathbf{16x^7}$ 8. $2^{-3} \cdot x^{-3} = 1/2^3x^3 = \mathbf{1/8x^3}$ 9. $2^2a^2 \cdot 3^2b^2 \cdot 5^2c^2 = 4a^2 \cdot 9b^2 \cdot 25c^2 = \mathbf{900a^2b^2c^2}$
10. $(2^{-2} \cdot x^{5(-2)})/(3^{-2} \cdot y^{2(-2)}) = (2^{-2} \cdot x^{-10})/(3^{-2} \cdot y^{-4}) = (3^2 \cdot y^4)/(2^2 \cdot x^{10}) = \mathbf{9y^4/4x^{10}}$ 11. $x^{4(3)} \cdot y^{5(3)} \cdot z^{8(3)} = \mathbf{x^{12}y^{15}z^{24}}$
12. $(x^{-3(-1)})/(3^{-1} \cdot y^{4(-1)}) = x^3/(3^{-1} \cdot y^{-4}) = 3^1x^3y^4/1 = \mathbf{3x^3y^4}$

Page by page detailed explanations in **Full Book WEBINAR**. Purchase online at www.Crazy-Brainz.com

Equations: Adding, Subtracting

When you add or subtract on one side of the equal sign (=)
YOU MUST DO THE SAME ON THE OTHER SIDE
OF THE EQUAL SIGN.
*(Ex: If you subtract 5 on the left side of the equal sign, you **MUST** subtract 5 on the right side of the equal sign).*

We will first use addition & subtraction
to CANCEL OUT numbers
and eventually get to "x = answer."

The end goal of solving equations is to find out what x or y (or any variable) equals.

How do you know to ADD or SUBTRACT?

Use the OPPOSITE sign of what you see.

For example: x + 5 = 6
The goal is to get x = answer so
CANCEL OUT the 5.

5 is being ADDED,
to cancel it out, SUBTRACT 5.

$$x + 5 = 6$$
$$\begin{aligned} x + 5 &= 6 \\ -5 &\;\; -5 \\ \hline x + 0 &= 1 \\ x &= 1 \end{aligned}$$

After subtracting 5 FROM BOTH SIDES, we have the answer, x = 1. +5 and -5 cancel each other out to equal zero, now the x is by itself on the left side of the equal sign. x = 1.

Always perform the OPPOSITE OPERATION in order to cancel out numbers.
If a number is being ***added***, SUBTRACT IT **to cancel it out.**
If a number is being ***subtracted***, ADD IT **to cancel it out.**

A. $x - 12 = 3$

$$\begin{aligned} x - 12 &= 3 \\ +12 &\;\; +12 \\ \hline x + 0 &= 15 \\ x &= 15 \end{aligned}$$

B. $8 = 15 + x$

$$\begin{aligned} 8 &= 15 + x \\ -15 &\;\; -15 \\ \hline -7 &= x \\ x &= -7 \end{aligned}$$

C. $-6 + x = 2$

$$\begin{aligned} -6 + x &= 2 \\ +6 &\;\; +6 \\ \hline x &= 8 \end{aligned}$$

A. Check the answer for x =15.
Plug 15 into the equation for x
and solve to see if it is true.
3 = 3 is true. x = 15 is confirmed.

$$\begin{aligned} x - 12 &= 3 \\ 15 - 12 &= 3 \\ 3 &= 3 \end{aligned}$$

B. Check the answer for x = -7.
Plug (- 7) into the equation for x
and solve to see if it is true.
8 = 8 is true. x = - 7 is confirmed.

$$\begin{aligned} 8 &= 15 + x \\ 8 &= 15 + (-7) \\ 8 &= 8 \end{aligned}$$

E. Variables AND numbers can BOTH be added or subtracted. In order to find what x equals, all of the x's must be on the same side of the equal sign.
The first step here is to cancel out 3x on the right side in order to get the x's on the LEFT SIDE ONLY, now we can solve for 1x = "some number." Next, subtract 4 from each side, leaving x = -12.

D. $5x + 9 = 4x$

$$\begin{aligned} 5x + 9 &= 4x \\ -4x &\;\; -4x \\ \hline 1x + 9 &= 0 \\ -9 &\;\; -9 \\ \hline x &= -9 \end{aligned}$$

E. $4x + 4 = 3x - 8$

$$\begin{aligned} 4x + 4 &= 3x - 8 \\ -3x &\;\; -3x \\ \hline 1x + 4 &= -8 \\ -4 &\;\; -4 \\ \hline x &= -12 \end{aligned}$$

It is ALWAYS a good idea to check your answer by plugging the value into the equation (ex. A and B).

More practice: Algebra Is Easy Part 1 SUCCESS BOOK (Workbook + Test Book)

Equations: Adding, Subtracting Practice

1. $x + 9 = 12$	2. $12 + x = -5$	3. $x - 4 = 5$
4. $3x - 2 = 2x + 1$	5. $9x + 4 = 8x - 5$	6. $7x + 4 = 6x + 6$
7. $x - 6 = 12$	8. $3 + x = 9$	9. $x - 15 = 25$

Written by April Chloe Terrazas

Practice Answers:

1. $x + 9 = 12$
   $-9 \quad -9$
   $\mathbf{x = 3}$

2. $12 + x = -5$
   $-12 \quad -12$
   $\mathbf{x = -17}$

3. $x - 4 = 5$
   $+4 \quad +4$
   $\mathbf{x = 9}$

4. $3x - 2 = 2x + 1$
   $-2x \quad -2x$
   $1x - 2 = 1$
   $+2 \quad +2$
   $\mathbf{x = 3}$

5. $9x + 4 = 8x - 5$
   $-8x \quad -8x$
   $1x + 4 = -5$
   $-4 \quad -4$
   $\mathbf{x = -9}$

6. $7x + 4 = 6x + 6$
   $-6x \quad -6x$
   $1x + 4 = 6$
   $-4 \quad -4$
   $\mathbf{x = 2}$

7. $x - 6 = 12$
   $+6 \quad +6$
   $\mathbf{x = 18}$

8. $3 + x = 9$
   $-3 \quad -3$
   $\mathbf{x = 6}$

9. $x - 15 = 25$
   $+15 \quad +15$
   $\mathbf{x = 40}$

Equations: Multiplying, Dividing

When you multiply or divide on one side of the equal sign (=)
YOU MUST DO THE SAME ON THE OTHER SIDE
OF THE EQUAL SIGN.

(Ex: If you divide by 4 on the left side of the equal sign, you ***MUST*** *divide by 4 on the right side of the equal sign).*

We will now use multiplication and division to CANCEL OUT numbers and eventually get to "x = answer."

The end goal of solving equations is to find out what x or y (or any variable) equals.

How do you know to MULTIPLY or DIVIDE?

Use the OPPOSITE sign of what you see.

For example: $4x = 24$
The goal is to get x = answer so I need to **CANCEL OUT the 4.**

4 is being MULTIPLIED by x, to cancel it out, DIVIDE by 4.

$$4x = 24$$
$$\frac{4x}{4} = \frac{24}{4}$$
$$x = 6$$

After dividing 4 FROM BOTH SIDES, we have the answer, x = 6. 4 divided by 4 cancel each other out to equal ONE, now the x is by itself on the left side of the equal sign. **x = 24 divided by 4, x = 6.**

Always perform the OPPOSITE OPERATION in order to cancel out numbers.
If a number is being ***multiplied***, DIVIDE IT **to cancel it out.**
If a number is being ***divided***, MULTIPLY IT **to cancel it out.**

A. $8x = 32$

$$\frac{8x}{8} = \frac{32}{8}$$ (①, ②)
$$1x = 4$$
$$x = 4$$

8 is being multiplied by x. To **cancel out the 8** and get ***x = answer***, **Step 1: do the OPPOSITE and DIVIDE** by 8, canceling the 8's to equal 1, **Step 2:** then divide by 8 on the other side of the equal sign. 32 divided by 8 = 4. **x = 4.**
("1x" and "x" are the same)

B. $\frac{x}{6} = 7$

$$6 \cdot \frac{x}{6} = 7 \cdot 6$$ (①, ②)
$$x = 42$$

x is being divided by 6. To **cancel out the 6** and get ***x = answer***, **Step 1: do the OPPOSITE and MULTIPLY** by 6, canceling the 6's to equal 1, **Step 2:** multiply by 6 on the other side of the equal sign. 7 times 6 = 42. **x = 42.**

C. $5x = 45$

$$\frac{5x}{5} = \frac{45}{5}$$ (①, ②)
$$1x = 9$$
$$x = 9$$

D. $\frac{x}{4} = 3$

$$4 \cdot \frac{x}{4} = 3 \cdot 4$$ (①, ②)
$$x = 12$$

E. $\frac{3}{5}x = 9$

Any whole number ca be written as itself over $9 = \frac{9}{1}$

$$\frac{5}{3} \cdot \frac{3}{5}x = \frac{9}{1} \cdot \frac{5}{3}$$ (①, ②)
$$\frac{15}{15} = 1$$
$$1x = \frac{45 \div 3}{3 \div 3} = \frac{15}{1}$$ (③ Reduce)
$$x = 15$$

x is being multiplied by $\frac{3}{5}$.
To **cancel out the fraction** and get ***x = answer***,
Step 1: do the OPPOSITE and DIVIDE by $\frac{3}{5}$.
Remember, dividing fractions means you MULTIPLY BY THE RECIPROCAL ($\frac{5}{3}$), **canceling the fractions** to equal $\frac{15}{15}$, **which equals 1x**.
Step 2: then multiply by the reciprocal ($\frac{5}{3}$) on the other side of the equal sign. $\frac{9}{1}$ times $\frac{5}{3} = \frac{45}{3}$
Step 3: reduce (**÷ by 3 on top and bottom**) **x = 15.**

Equations: Multiplying, Dividing Practice

1. $\frac{x}{5} = 7$	2. $12 = \frac{x}{2}$	3. $\frac{x}{8} = 4$
4. $4x = 16$	5. $-9x = 81$	6. $-3x = -36$
7. $\frac{x}{6} = 10$	8. $12x = 72$	9. $\frac{x}{7} = 5$

Written by April Chloe Terrazas

Practice Answers:

1. x/5 = 7
multiply by 5 both sides
5x/5 = 35
5x/5 reduces to 1x
x = 35

2. 12 = x/2
multiply by 2 both sides
24 = 2x/2
2x/2 reduces to 1x
x = 24

3. x/8 = 4
multiply by 8 both sides
8x/8 = 32
8x/8 reduces to 1x
x = 32

4. 4x = 16
divide by 4 both sides
4x/4 = 4
4x/4 reduces to 1x
x = 4

5. - 9x = 81
divide by - 9 both sides
- 9x/ - 9 = - 9
- 9x/- 9 reduces to +1x
x = - 9

6. - 3x = - 36
divide by - 3 both sides
- 3x/ - 3 = + 12
- 3x/ - 3 reduces to 1x
x = + 12

7. x/6 = 10
multiply by 6 both sides
6x/6 = 60
6x/6 reduces to 1x
x = 60

8. 12x = 72
divide by 12 both sides
12x/12 = 6
12x/12 reduces to 1x
x = 6

9. x/7 = 5
multiply by 7 both sides
7x/7 = 35
7x/7 reduces to 1x
x = 35

Equations: Multi-Step

Whatever operation you do on one side of the equal sign (=) YOU MUST DO ON THE OTHER SIDE OF THE EQUAL SIGN.

*(Ex: If you multiply 5 on one side of the equal sign, you **MUST** multiply 5 on the other side).*

We will now use adding, subtracting, multiplying and dividing to solve MULTI-STEP problems.

The end goal of solving equations (even large, complex equations!) is to find out what the variable equals.

Steps for Solving Multi-Step Equations:

1. Simplify as much as possible

2. Add/subtract

3. Multiply/divide

Always CHECK YOUR ANSWER!

Don't forget PEMDAS and distribution.

If you see 3(2x + 5), you must DISTRIBUTE FIRST as part of *Step 1: Simplify*

Always perform the OPPOSITE OPERATION in order to cancel out numbers.

If a number is being ***added***, SUBTRACT IT **to cancel it out.**

If a number is being ***subtracted***, ADD IT **to cancel it out.**

If a number is being ***multiplied***, DIVIDE IT **to cancel it out.**

If a number is being ***divided***, MULTIPLY IT **to cancel it out.**

RS= right side
LS = left side

Step 1: Distribute 3 to 2x + 5.

Step 2: Combine LIKE TERMS, 4x + 6x = 10x

Step 3: Subtract 7x from the RS.

Step 4: Subtract 7x from the LS.

Step 5: Subtract 15 from the LS.

Step 6: Subtract 15 from the RS.

Step 7: Divide by 3 on the LS.

Step 8: Divide by 3 on the RS.

-6 divided by 3 = -2

x = -2.

$$4x + 3(2x + 5) = 7x + 9$$

$$4x + 3(2x + 5) = 7x + 9 \quad (1)$$

$$4x + 6x + 15 = 7x + 9 \quad (2)$$

$$10x + 15 = 7x + 9$$

$$(4)\ -7x \qquad (3)\ -7x$$

$$3x + 15 = 9$$

$$(5)\ -15 \qquad -15\ (6)$$

$$(7)\ \frac{3x}{3} = \frac{-6}{3}\ (8)$$

$$x = -2$$

More practice: Algebra Is Easy Part 1 SUCCESS BOOK (Workbook + Test Book)

Equations: Multi-Step Practice

1. $8x + 6 = 30$
2. $5x + 4 = 2x + 13$
3. $4x - 2 = 10$
4. $3(2x + 3) = 12$
5. $5(x - 1) = 15 + 3x$
6. $8x + 3 = 19$
7. $2x - 6 + 4x = 2(5x - 1)$
8. $7x + 4(2x + 2) = 11x - 12$

Written by April Chloe Terrazas

Practice Answers:

1. $8x + 6 = 30$
   - $-6 \quad -6$
   - $8x = 24$
   - $\frac{8x}{8} = \frac{24}{8}$
   - $x = 3$

2. $5x + 4 = 2x + 13$
   - $-2x \quad -2x$
   - $3x + 4 = 13$
   - $-4 \quad -4$
   - $3x = 9$
   - $\frac{3x}{3} = \frac{9}{3}$
   - $x = 3$

3. $4x - 2 = 10$
   - $+2 \quad +2$
   - $4x = 12$
   - $\frac{4x}{4} = \frac{12}{4}$
   - $x = 3$

4. $3(2x + 3) = 12$
   - $6x + 9 = 12$
   - $-9 \quad -9$
   - $\frac{6x}{6} = \frac{3}{6} \frac{\div 3}{\div 3} = \frac{1}{2}$
   - $x = \frac{1}{2}$

5. $5(x - 1) = 15 + 3x$
   - $5x - 5 = 15 + 3x$
   - $-3x \quad -3x$
   - $2x - 5 = 15$
   - $+5 \quad +5$
   - $2x = 20$
   - $\frac{2x}{2} = \frac{20}{2}$
   - $x = 10$

6. $8x + 3 = 19$
   - $-3 \quad -3$
   - $8x = 16$
   - $\frac{8x}{8} = \frac{16}{8}$
   - $x = 2$

7. $2x - 6 + 4x = 2(5x - 1)$
   - $6x - 6 = 10x - 2$
   - $-6x \quad -6x$
   - $-6 = 4x - 2$
   - $+2 \quad +2$
   - $-4 = 4x$
   - $\frac{-4}{4} = \frac{4x}{4}$
   - $-1 = x$
   - Same
   - $x = -1$

8. $7x + 4(2x + 2) = 11x - 12$
   - $7x + 8x + 8 = 11x - 12$
   - $15x + 8 = 11x - 12$
   - $-11x \quad -11x$
   - $4x + 8 = -12$
   - $-8 \quad -8$
   - $4x = -20$
   - $\frac{4x}{4} = \frac{-20}{4}$
   - $x = -5$

Absolute Value Equations

Step 1: Isolate the absolute value.

This means adding, subtracting, multiplying, dividing, doing what is necessary to get the absolute value portion on one side of the equal sign ALONE.

Step 2: Once the absolute value is alone, solve TWO SEPARATE EQUATIONS, the first = + #, the second = - #. **In this example, set the equation equal to 4 and another equal to - 4.** *Because this is "absolute value", you must account for the possibility of a positive AND negative outcome.*

Absolute value equations will usually have TWO ANSWERS.

A. $3|2x+6|-7=5$

$+7 \quad +7$

$\frac{3|2x+6|}{3}=\frac{12}{3}$

$|2x+6|=4$

2 equations

$2x+6=+4$	$2x+6=-4$
$2x+6=4$	$2x+6=-4$
$-6 \quad -6$	$-6 \quad -6$
$\frac{2x}{2}=\frac{-2}{2}$	$\frac{2x}{2}=\frac{-10}{2}$
$x=-1$	$x=-5$

$x=-1$ AND $x=-5$

Check both answers

x = -1

x = 5

$3|2(-1)+6|-7=5$

$3|-2+6|-7=5$

$|4|=4$ $\quad 3|4|-7=5$

$3\cdot 4-7=5$

$12-7=5$

$5=5$ ✓

$3|2(-5)+6|-7=5$

$3|-10+6|-7=5$

$|-4|=4$ $\quad 3|-4|-7=5$

$3\cdot 4-7=5$

$12-7=5$

$5=5$ ✓

B. $4|x|=20$

$\frac{4|x|}{4}=\frac{20}{4}$

$|x|=5$

$x=5$ $\quad x=-5$

C. $|5x+10|=0$

$|5x+10|=0$

$5x+10=0 \quad 5x+10=0$

Same equation, no +/- option

1 ANSWER

$5x+10=0$

$-10 \quad -10$

$\frac{5x}{5}=\frac{-10}{5}$

$x=-2$

More practice: Algebra Is Easy Part 1 SUCCESS BOOK (Workbook + Test Book)

Absolute Value Equations Practice

1. $|x| = 3$

2. $|2x| = 10$

3. $|4x| = 28$

4. $2|x - 1| = 10$

5. $3|2x + 6| = 9$

6. $8|5x - 3| = 24$

7. $7|2x + 5| + 3 = 10$

1. $|x| = 3$

$x = 3 \quad x = -3$

2. $|2x| = 10$

$\frac{2x}{2} = \frac{10}{2} \quad \frac{2x}{2} = \frac{-10}{2}$

$x = 5 \quad x = -5$

3. $|4x| = 28$

$\frac{4x}{4} = \frac{28}{4} \quad \frac{4x}{4} = \frac{-28}{4}$

$x = 7 \quad x = -7$

4. $\frac{2|x-1|}{2} = \frac{10}{2}$

$|x-1| = 5$

$x - 1 = 5 \quad x - 1 = -5$

$+1 \quad +1 \qquad +1 \quad +1$

$x = 6 \quad x = -4$

5. $\frac{3|2x+6|}{3} = \frac{9}{3}$

$|2x+6| = 3$

$2x + 6 = 3 \quad 2x + 6 = -3$

$-6 \quad -6 \qquad -6 \quad -6$

$\frac{2x}{2} = \frac{-3}{2} \quad \frac{2x}{2} = \frac{-9}{2}$

$x = -\frac{3}{2} \quad x = -\frac{9}{2}$

6. $\frac{8|5x-3|}{8} = \frac{24}{8}$

$|5x-3| = 3$

$5x - 3 = 3 \quad 5x - 3 = -3$

$+3 \quad +3 \qquad +3 \quad +3$

$\frac{5x}{5} = \frac{6}{5} \quad \frac{5x}{5} = \frac{0}{5}$

$x = \frac{6}{5} \quad x = 0$

7. $7|2x+5| + 3 = 10$

$-3 \quad -3$

$\frac{7|2x+5|}{7} = \frac{7}{7}$

$|2x+5| = 1$

$2x + 5 = 1 \quad 2x + 5 = -1$

$-5 \quad -5 \qquad -5 \quad -5$

$\frac{2x}{2} = \frac{-4}{2} \quad \frac{2x}{2} = \frac{-6}{2}$

$x = -2 \quad x = -3$

You =

Awesome

Graphing on Coordinate Grid (x, y)

Graphing is based on using the x and y axis. To locate a coordinate, simply count how far **left or right the point is from the origin**, this is the **x-coordinate**. Then, count how far **up or down the point is from the origin**, this is the **y-coordinate**.

A "coordinate pair", or a "point," is ALWAYS in the form **(x, y)**.

The starting point (center) of the graph is called the **origin**. The coordinate of the origin is **(0,0)**.

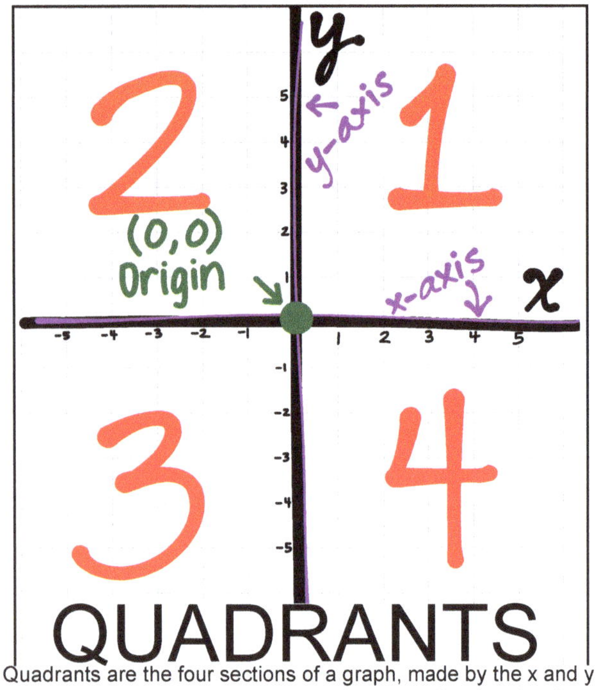

Quadrants are the four sections of a graph, made by the x and y axes intersecting. You may also see them as Q1, Q2, Q3, Q4.

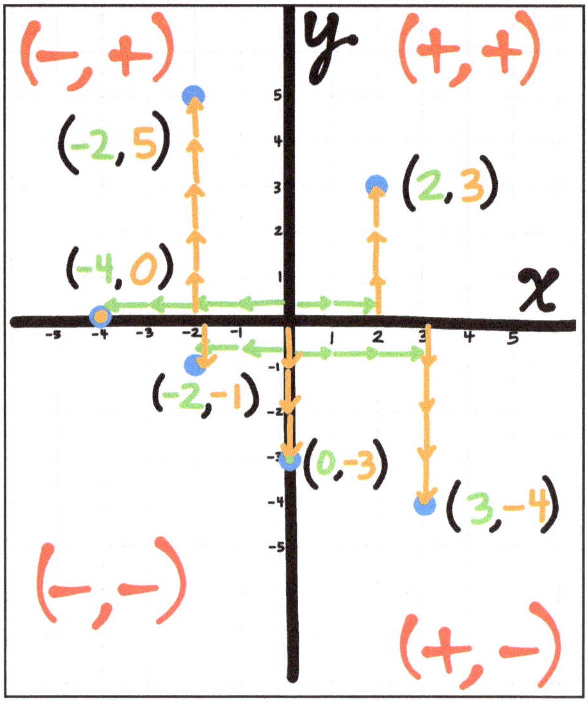

1.

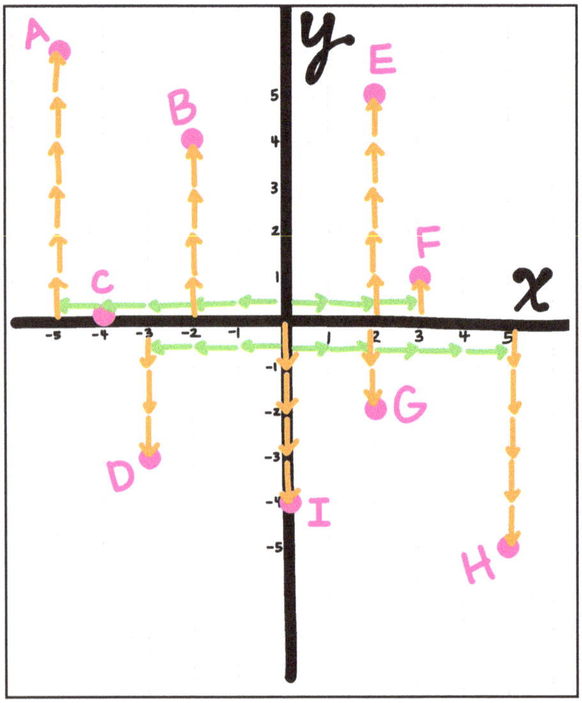

a. Label the points on the coordinate grid (x,y)
b. Name the points in Q1, Q2, Q3 and Q4

2.

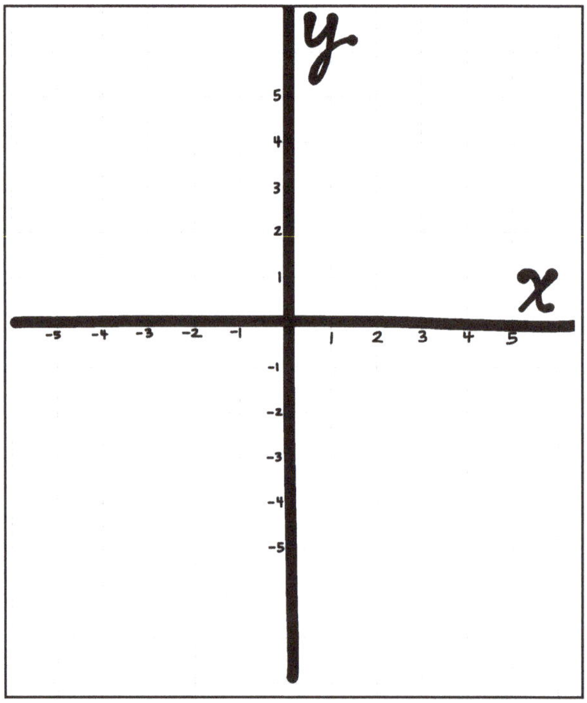

Label the following points on the coordinate grid.

A (3, 0) B (4, 5) C (-1, 2) D (0, 4)
E (-3, -2) F (3, -4) G (5, 5) H (2, -4)

Practice 1 Answers
A (-5, 6) B (-2, 4) C (-4, 0) D (-3, -3) E (2, 5) F (3, 1) G (2, -2) H (5, -5) I (0, -4) Q1: E, F Q2: A, B Q3: D Q4: G, H
Points ON the x or y axis are NOT in any quadrant.

Graphing a Linear Equation with a Table

How to graph a linear equation using A TABLE.

A linear equation is a formula for finding points on a graph.

Plug in values for x (you choose!) into the formula (*equation*) and **solve for y**.

$$y = 3x + 1$$

I choose to plug in -2, -1, 0, 1, and 2. You may choose any points you like! I recommend (for graphing purposes) to choose small values close to 0 so all of the points will fit easier on a simple graph.
It is recommended to plot at least 3 points. The more points, the more accurate the graph.

x	-2	-1	0	1	2
y	3(-2) + 1 = -5	3(-1) + 1 = -2	3(0) + 1 = 1	3(1) + 1 = 4	3(2) + 1 = 7

Step 1:
make a table

Step 2:
choose values to plug in for X

Step 3:
solve the equation for y, using the value you plugged in for X.

Step 4:
Make coordinates (x, y) out the of table and plot the points.

Step 5:
Connect the points with a line.

$y = 3x + 1$

Table →

x	y
-2	-5
-1	-2
0	1
1	4
2	7

(2,7)
(1,4)
(0,1)
(-1,-2)
(-2,-5)

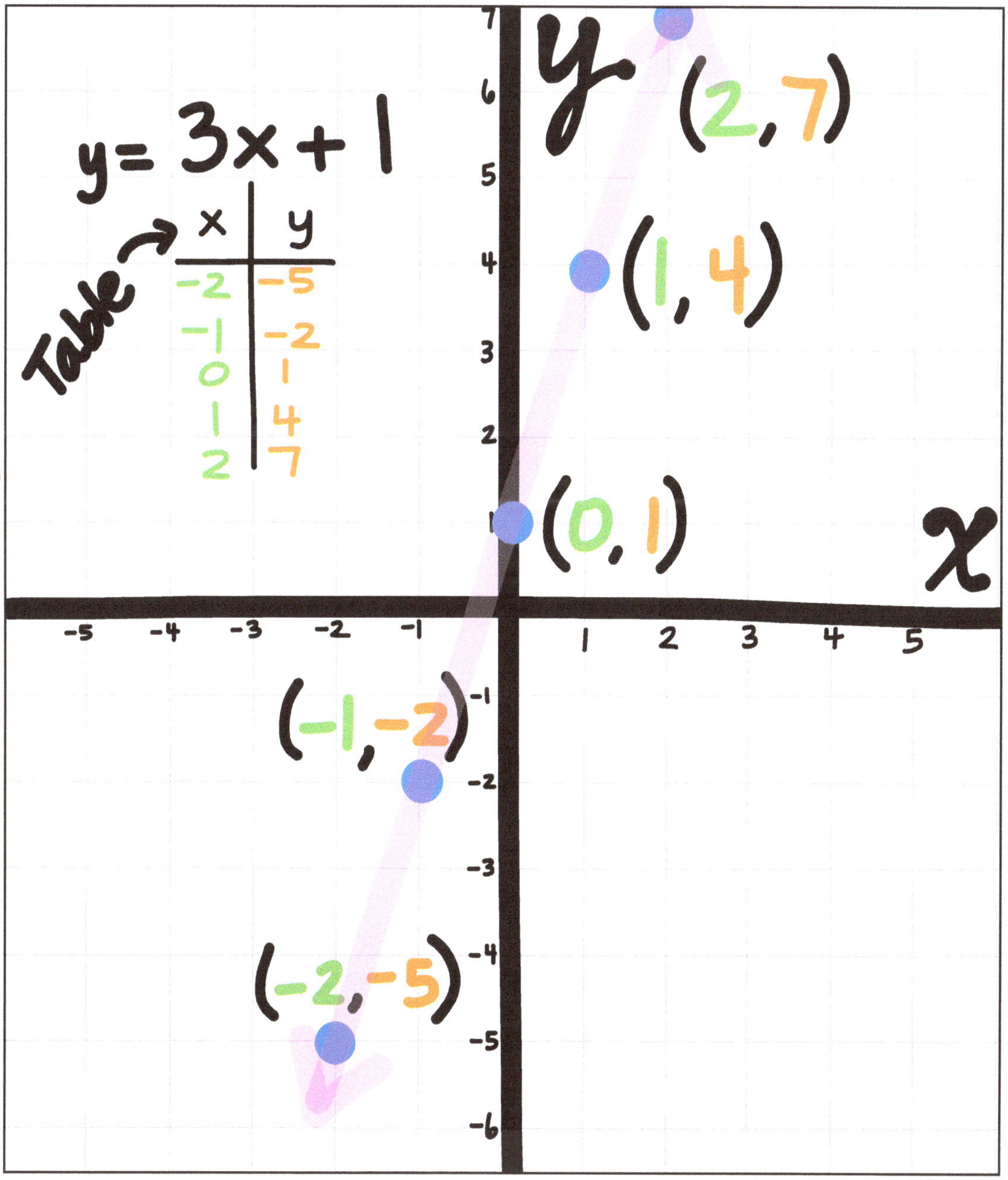

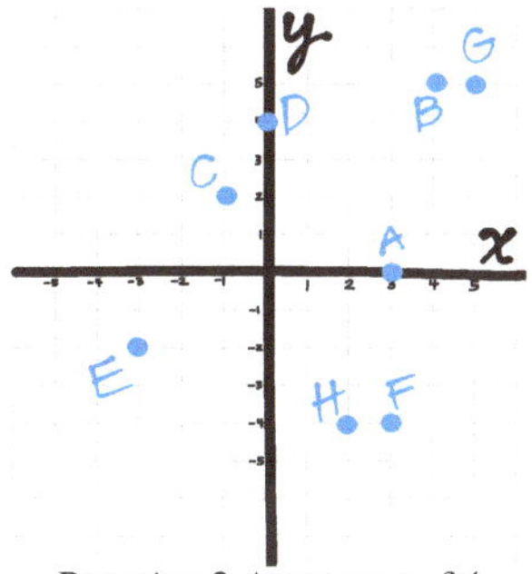

Practice 2 Answers p. 34

Graphing a Linear Equation (Line)

How to graph a linear equation using SLOPE-INTERCEPT FORM: y = mx + b

m = SLOPE = RISE (or FALL)/RUN.
This tells you how many units to go up or down (RISE or FALL) and then how many units to go RIGHT (run).

A positive slope will RISE.
A negative slope will FALL.

b = y-intercept.
This is the point where the line crosses the y-axis and it is also a good starting point for graphing a line. Plot this point (1), then use the slope to get to the next point (2), and again use the slope to get to the third point (3).

Graph y = 2x + 2. First, plot the y-intercept, +2 (1). Then, use the slope to get to the next point. Rise 2, run 1 and plot a point (2). Use the slope again to get to the third point, rise 2, run 1 (3).

Then connect the points with a line (4). YOU DID IT!

Positive slopes go
UP HILL
from left to right.

Negative slopes go
DOWN HILL
from left to right.

It is recommended to
find at least 3 points
for an accurate line.

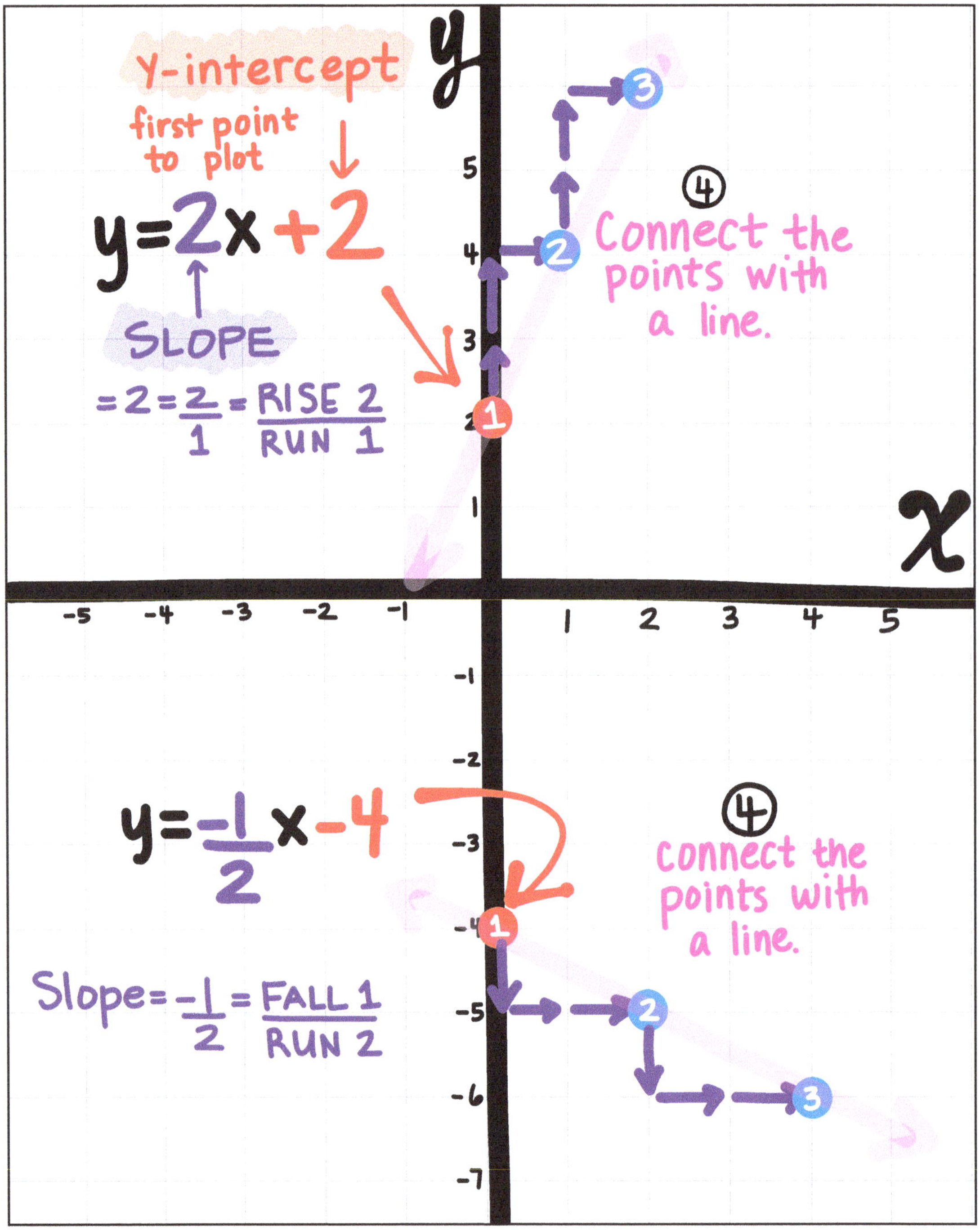

Example 2:
Graph $y = {}^{-1}/_{2}\,x - 4$.
Y-intercept is -4.
First point at y = -4.
Use slope to get to next points. Fall 1, run 2.
Fall 1, run 2.

Fall because slope is negative.

m = slope

b = y-intercept

Graphing a Linear Equation Practice

1 - 3. Graph the following linear equations using A TABLE

$y = 2x - 1$ $\qquad$ $y = \frac{1}{3}x + 2$ $\qquad$ $y = -2x + 1$

1.

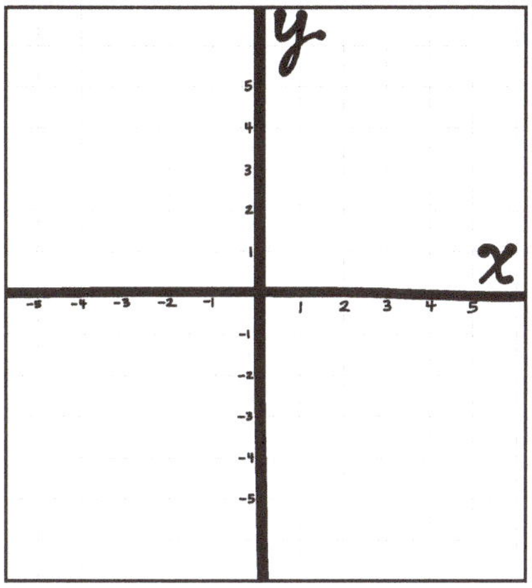

2.

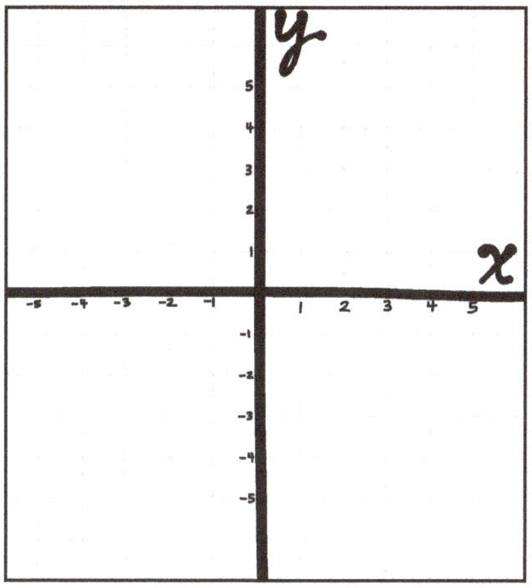

3.

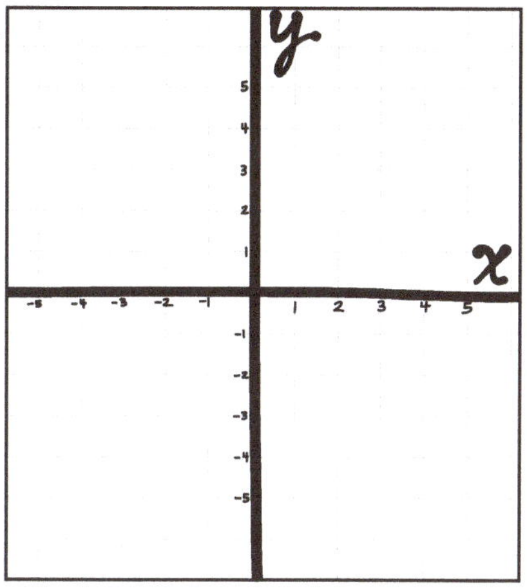

4 - 6. Graph the following linear equations using SLOPE-INTERCEPT FORM.

$y = 4x - 3$ $\qquad$ $y = \frac{1}{2}x + 2$ $\qquad$ $y = -3x + 4$

4.

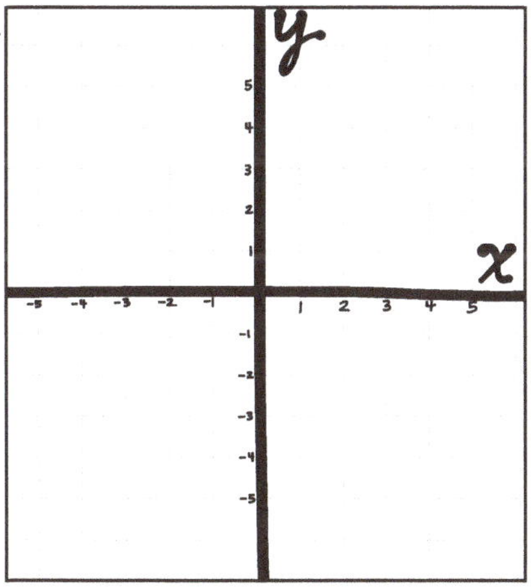

5.

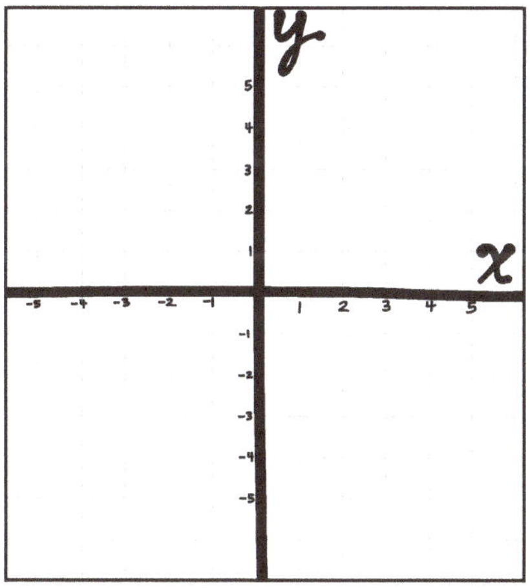

6.

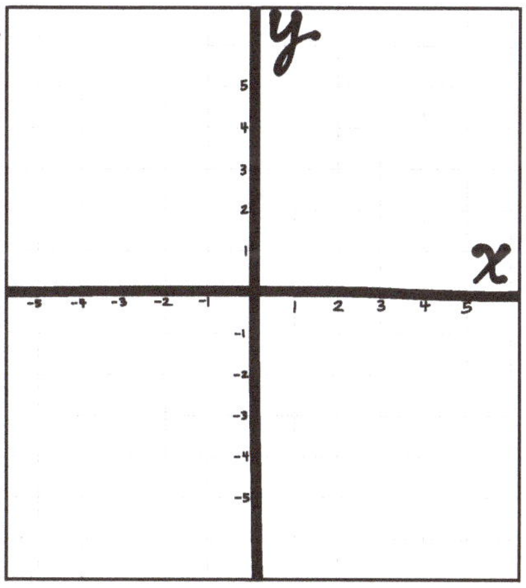

Written by April Chloe Terrazas

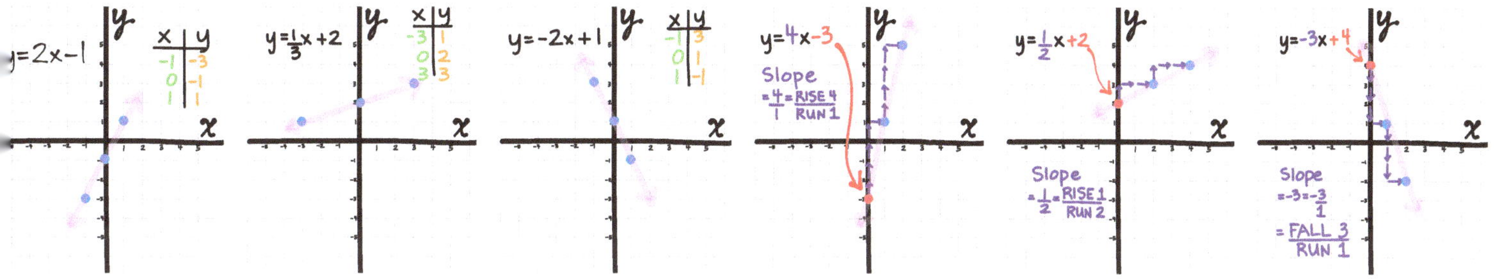

Graphing Horizontal & Vertical Lines

How to graph equations that have only X, or only Y:

For example:	$y = 4$	$y = -2$	$x = 1$	$x = -5$

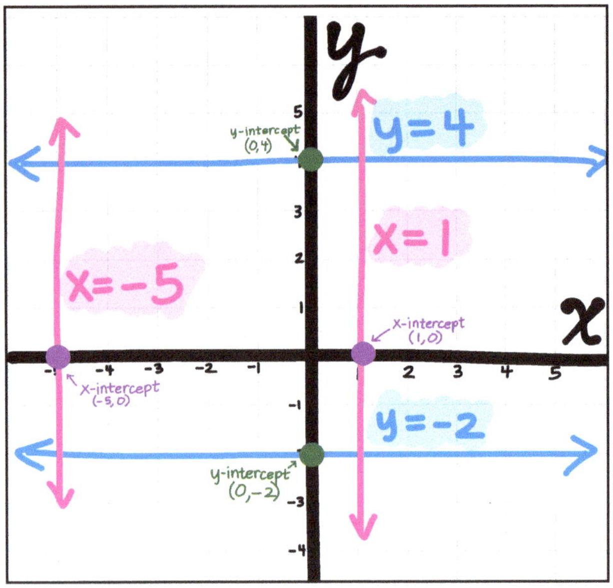

Y = HORIZONTAL LINE through the y value

X = VERTICAL LINE through the x value

In horizontal lines, ***the slope is ZERO***. Imagine incline on a treadmill. Flat road has a ZERO% incline.

A horizontal line has ONLY a Y-INTERCEPT. It ONLY crosses the y-axis.

The **y-intercept** (*where the line crosses the y-axis*) of $y = -2$ is at **(0, -2)**. The y-intercept of $y = 4$ is at **(0, 4)**.

In veritcal lines, ***THERE IS NO SLOPE***. It is not possible to walk on a treadmill perpendicular to the ground.

A vertical line has ONLY an X-INTERCEPT. It ONLY crosses the x-axis.

The **x-intercept** (*where the line crosses the x-axis*) of $x = -5$ is **(-5, 0)**. The x-intercept of $x = 1$ is **(1, 0)**.

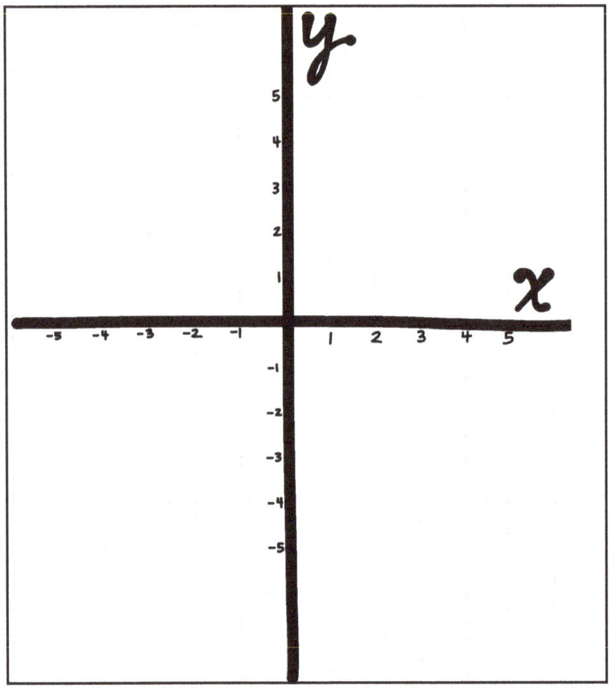

Graph the following equations on the grid:

a. $y = -4$ b. $y = -1$ c. $y = 3$

d. $x = -3$ e. $x = 0$ f. $x = 4$

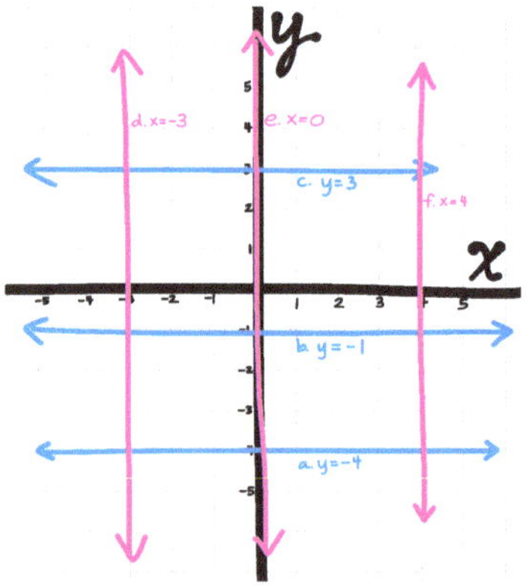

More practice: Algebra Is Easy Part 1 SUCCESS BOOK (Workbook + Test Book)

Finding x and y Intercepts

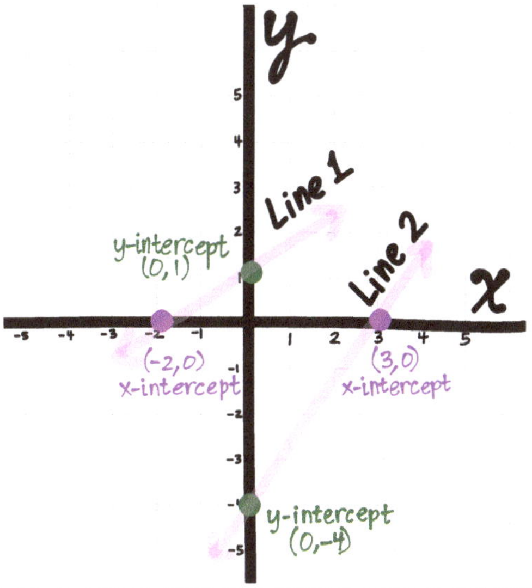

The **x-intercept** is where the line crosses the x-axis.
This occurs when y = 0.

y = 0 IS the X-AXIS.

The x-intercept in line 1 is at (-2, 0).
The x-intercept in line 2 is at (3, 0).

The **y-intercept** is where the line crosses the y-axis.
This occurs when x = 0.

x = 0 IS the Y-AXIS.

The y-intercept in line 1 is at (0, 1).
The y-intercept in line 2 is at (0, -4).

How to find x and y intercepts <u>WITHOUT A GRAPH</u>

Find the x and y-intercepts of the following equation, and graph.

$$2x + 6y = 12$$

Find x-intercept

x-intercept is where y = 0.

Plug in y = 0 and solve for x.

$2x + 6(0) = 12$

$2x + 0 = 12$

$2x = 12$

$\mathbf{x = 6}$

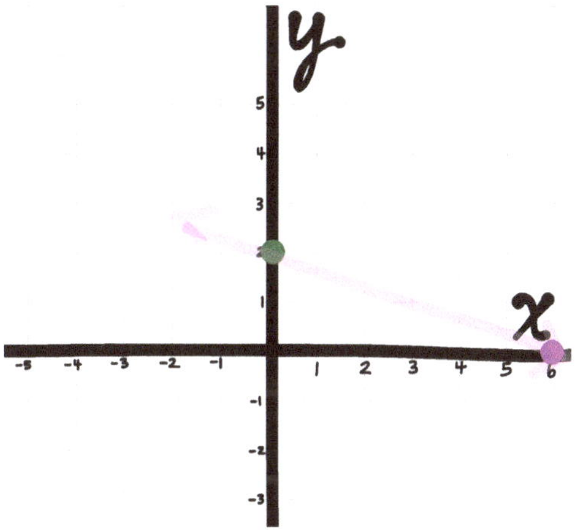

Find y-intercept

y-intercept is where x = 0.

Plug in x = 0 and solve for y.

$2(0) + 6y = 12$

$0 + 6y = 12$

$6y = 12$

$\mathbf{y = 2}$

Written by April Chloe Terrazas

Practice: Find the x and y intercepts of each, graph.

1. $5x + 3y = 15$

2. $8x + 4y = 24$

3. $3x + 4y = 12$

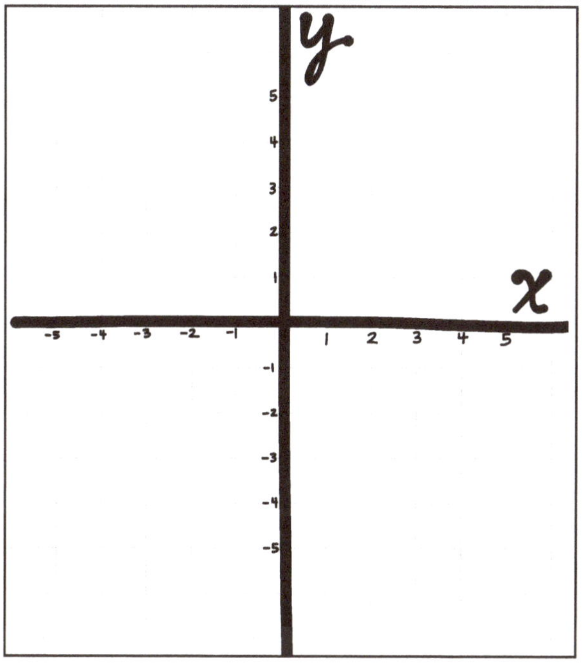

Practice Answers: 1. x = 3, y = 5 2. x = 3, y = 6 3. x = 4, y = 3

Finding SLOPE from two points

Find the slope of a line that passes through the points (-2, -1) and (1, 5).

Slope is found by finding the difference between the two y values, divided by the difference of the two x-values.

We will call *POINT 1* (-2, -1), and *POINT 2* (1, 5).

Remember, slope = m = RISE/RUN.
y must ALWAYS be in the numerator.
x must ALWAYS be in the denominator.

$$\text{Slope} = m = \frac{y_2 - y_1}{x_2 - x_1} = \frac{5 - (-1)}{1 - (-2)} = \frac{6}{3} = 2$$

m = + 2

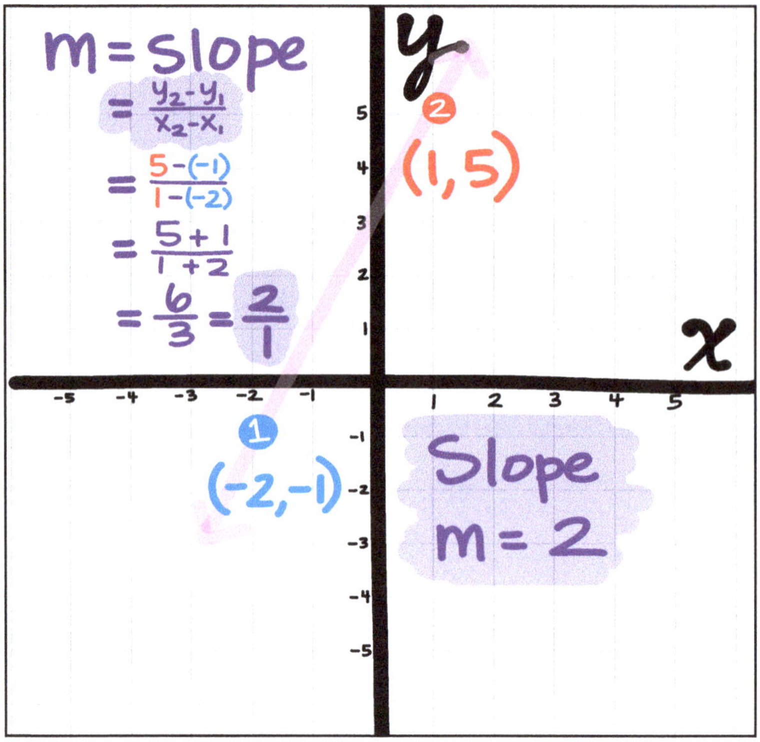

Remember, a horizontal (y = #) line has a slope of ZERO. A vertical line (x = #) has NO SLOPE.

Find the slope of the horizontal line that passes through the points (2, 3) and (4, 3).

We will call *POINT 1* (2, 3), and *POINT 2* (4, 3).

$$\text{Slope} = m = \frac{y_2 - y_1}{x_2 - x_1} = \frac{3 - (3)}{4 - (2)} = \frac{0}{2} = 0$$

m = 0

Find the slope of the vertical line that passes through the points (5, 1) and (5, 4).

We will call *POINT 1* (5, 1), and *POINT 2* (5, 4).

$$\text{Slope} = m = \frac{y_2 - y_1}{x_2 - x_1} = \frac{4 - (1)}{5 - (5)} = \frac{7}{0} = \text{UNDEFINED (NO SLOPE)}$$

m = UNDEFINED

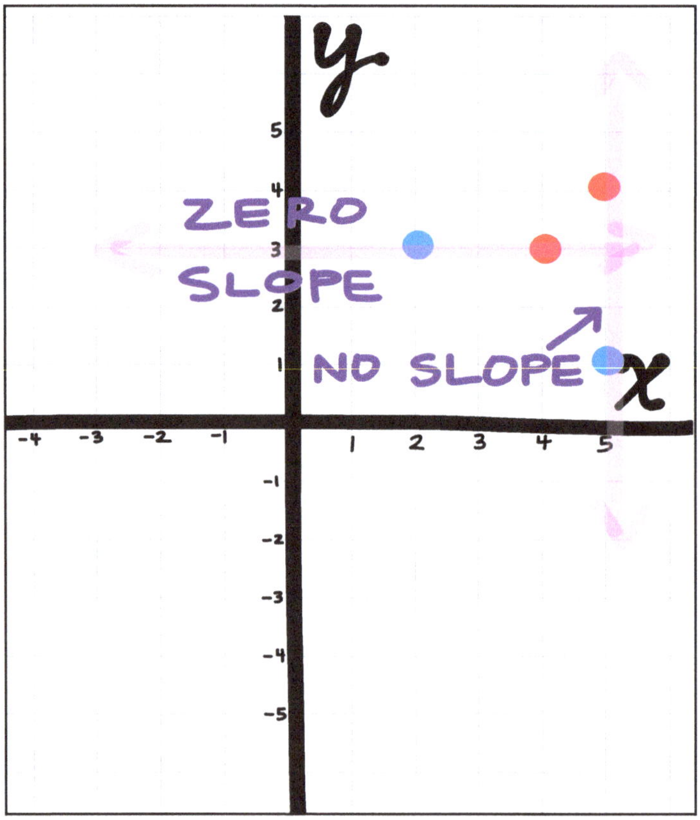

Practice: Find the slope of the line that passes through two given points.

1. (4, 7) and (5, 9)
2. (-2, -1) and (4, 6)
3. (-3, 0) and (3, 2)
4. (-5, 3) and (-5, -6)

Practice Answers:
1. m = 2
2. m = 7/6
3. m = 1/3
4. m = undefined

More practice: Algebra Is Easy Part 1 SUCCESS BOOK (Workbook + Test Book)

Slope-Intercept Form $y = mx + b$

The equations below are already in slope-intercept form. Sometimes, you have to re-write an equation to put it into slope intercept form, $y = mx + b$.

$y = 2x + 1$	slope = 2	y - intercept = + 1
$y = -x - 4$	slope = -1	y - intercept = - 4
$y = 1/3\ x + 3$	slope = 1/3	y - intercept = + 3

Write the equations in slope-intercept form:

a. $2x + 4y = 8$ b. $3x - 2y = 12$

c. $5y + x = 15$ d. $-4x - 2y = 10$

a. $2x + 4y = 8$
$-2x \qquad -2x$
$\frac{4y}{4} = \frac{-2x}{4} + \frac{8}{4}$
$\boxed{y = -\tfrac{1}{2}x + 2}$

b. $3x - 2y = 12$
$-3x \qquad -3x$
$\frac{-2y}{-2} = \frac{-3x}{-2} + \frac{12}{-2}$
$\boxed{y = \tfrac{3}{2}x - 6}$

c. $5y + x = 15$
$-x \qquad -x$
$\frac{5y}{5} = \frac{-x}{5} + \frac{15}{5}$
$\boxed{y = -\tfrac{1}{5}x + 3}$

d. $-4x - 2y = 10$
$+4x \qquad +4x$
$\frac{-2y}{-2} = \frac{4x}{-2} + \frac{10}{-2}$
$\boxed{y = -2x - 5}$

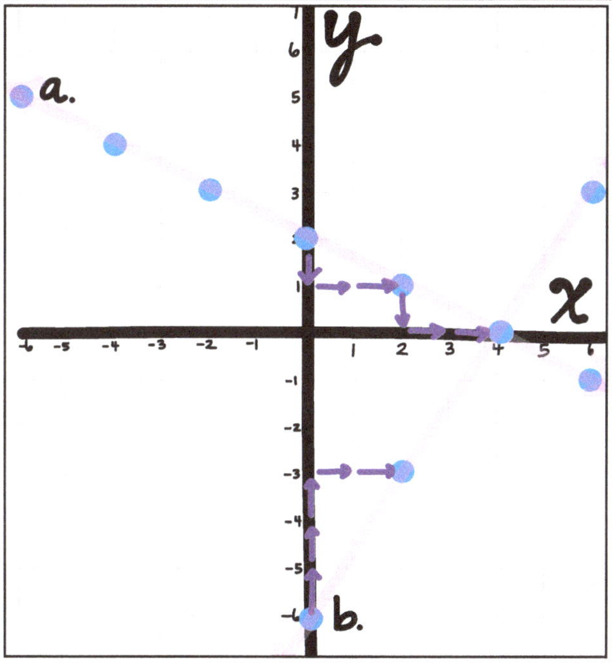

a. $y = -1/2\ x + 2$ m = - 1/2   b = + 2   b. $y = 3/2\ x - 6$ m = 3/2   b = -6

Begin by plotting "b" (y-intercept), then use slope to get other points.

Practice: Rewrite the following equations in slope-intercept form. Name the slope (m) and the y-intercept (b).

1. $2x + 6y = 12$ 2. $3x - 2y = 24$ 3. $12x + 5y = 2x + 10$

4. $8y = 4x - 16$ 5. $4y = -8x + 12$ 6. $2y + 3x = 7x + 6$

Practice Answers:

1. $2x + 6y = 12$
$-2x \qquad -2x$
$\frac{6y}{6} = \frac{-2x}{6} + \frac{12}{6}$
$\boxed{y = -\tfrac{1}{3}x + 2}$

2. $3x - 2y = 24$
$-3x \qquad -3x$
$\frac{-2y}{-2} = \frac{-3x}{-2} + \frac{24}{-2}$
$\boxed{y = \tfrac{3}{2}x - 12}$

3. $12x + 5y = 2x + 10$
$-12x \qquad -12x$
$\frac{5y}{5} = \frac{-10x}{5} + \frac{10}{5}$
$\boxed{y = -2x + 2}$

4. $\frac{8y}{8} = \frac{4x}{8} - \frac{16}{8}$
$\boxed{y = \tfrac{1}{2}x - 2}$

5. $\frac{4y}{4} = \frac{-8x}{4} + \frac{12}{4}$
$\boxed{y = -2x + 3}$

6. $2y + 3x = 7x + 6$
$-3x \quad -3x$
$\frac{2y}{2} = \frac{4x}{2} + \frac{6}{2}$
$\boxed{y = 2x + 3}$

1. m = -1/3	b = + 2
2. m = 3/2	b = - 12
3. m = - 2	b = + 2
4. m = 1/2	b = - 2
5. m = - 2	b = + 5
6. m = 2	b = + 3

Written by April Chloe Terrazas

Point-Slope Form $y - y_1 = m(x - x_1)$

Just like Slope-Intercept Form gives the slope and y-intercept in the equation, Point-Slope Form gives a point to plot and the slope for getting other points.

Both forms allow for easy graphing.

(x_1, y_1) is the point you INSERT INTO THE EQUATION.

For example: Write the equation of the line containing the given point and slope. (3, 4) m = 2

(3, 4) m = 2

Using the formula **$y - y_1 = m(x - x_1)$**, plug in the values of x and y from the given point, and the value of the slope. Done.

y - 4 = 2 (x - 3)

y - 4 = 2 (x - 3)

Transitioning from *POINT-SLOPE* to *SLOPE-INTERCEPT*.

Simply distribute and simplify point-slope form to get slope intercept form (y = mx + b).

Write the following equation in slope-intercept form.

y - 4 = 2 (x - 3)

distribute the 2 to (x - 3)

y - 4 = 2x - 6

+4 +4

y = 2x - 2

m = 2

b = - 2

To graph point-slope form, plot the given point and use slope to get additional points

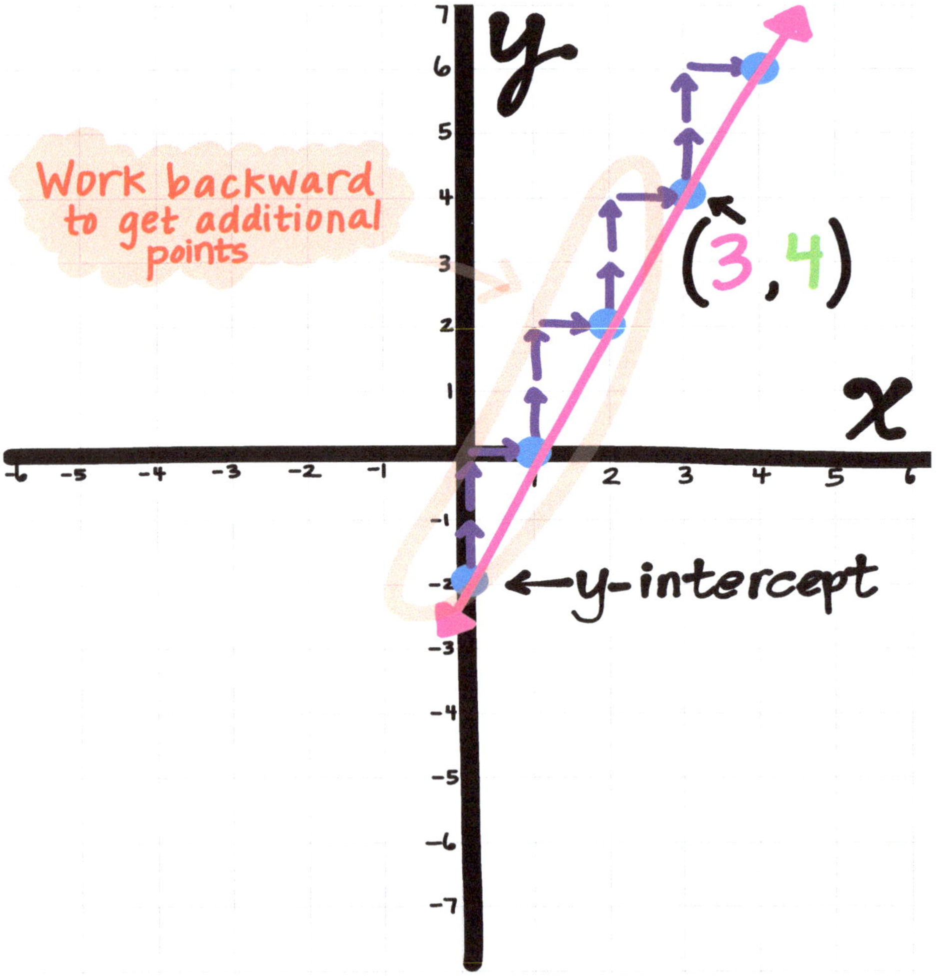

What if ONLY 2 points are given, and no slope?

Use the two points to FIND SLOPE.

For example:
Write the equation of the line containing the given points. (2, 3) (6, 5)

$$\text{Slope} = m = \frac{y_2 - y_1}{x_2 - x_1} = \frac{5 - (3)}{6 - (2)} = \frac{2}{4} = \frac{1}{2}$$

m = ½

Now, choose ONE of the two given points and, with slope, and plug them into point-slope form. I choose (2, 3).

y - 3 = 1/2 (x - 2)

Point-Slope Practice

Practice:

Write the equation of the line containing the given point and slope in point-slope form.

1. (1, 4)   m = 3

2. (-3, 5)   m = -1

3. (0, -1)   m = 6

4. (2, 7)   m = -1/2

Write the equation of the line containing the given points in point-slope form.

5. (4, 5) and (7, 8)

6. (0, 1) and (3, 6)

7. (-3, - 4) and (-1, 0)

8. (-2, 4) and (3, -6)

Written by April Chloe Terrazas

Practice Answers: 1. $y - 4 = 3(x - 1)$

2. $y - 5 = -1(x - (-3))$ $y - 5 = -1(x + 3)$

3. $y - (-1) = 6(x - 0)$ $y + 1 = 6(x)$

4. $y - 7 = -1/2(x - 2)$

5. slope $= \frac{8-5}{7-4} = \frac{3}{3} = 1$, $y - 5 = 1(x - 4)$

6. slope $= \frac{6-1}{3-0} = \frac{5}{3}$, $y - 1 = \frac{5}{3}(x - 0)$

7. slope $= \frac{0-(-4)}{(-1)-(-3)} = \frac{0+4}{(-1)+3} = \frac{4}{2} = 2$

$y - 0 = 2(x - (-1))$ $y = 2(x + 1)$

8. slope $= \frac{-6-4}{3-(-2)} = \frac{-10}{3+2} = \frac{-10}{5} = -2$

$y - 4 = -2(x - (-2))$ $y - 4 = -2(x + 2)$

Parallel and Perpendicular Lines

**Review BOTH pages 44 and 45 before beginning practice on p. 44.*

Parallel lines NEVER CROSS.
They are like the two rails of a railroad.
Always the same distance apart,
always the **same slope**.

For example: Find the parallel slope to $m = 3/4$

Parallel lines have the SAME SLOPE, therefore,
the parallel slope to m = 3/4 is $\mathbf{m = 3/4}$

Perpendicular lines ALWAYS CROSS.
Perpendicular lines cross specifically at a 90 degree angle.
Slopes of perpendicular lines are the
negative reciprocal of each other.

For example: Find the perpendicular slope to $m = 1/2$

Find the negative reciprocal (or flip) = $-2/1 = -2$. $\mathbf{m = -2}$

A.

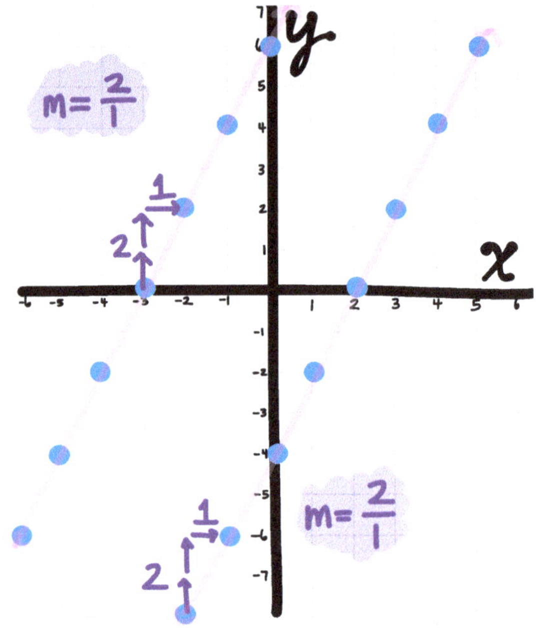

A.

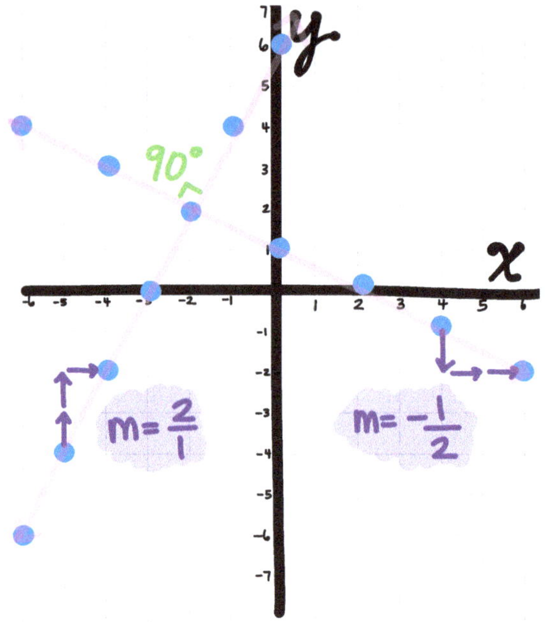

Examples of parallel lines:

A. y = 2x + 6
y = 2x - 4

B. y = - 2/3 x
y = - 2/3 x - 1

C. y = - 2x + 12
y = - 2x - 7

D. y = 5/6 x + 3
y = 5/6 x - 2

Examples of perpendicular lines:

A. y = 2x + 6
y = - 1/2x - 1

B. y = -2/3 x
y = 3/2 x - 1

C. y = -2x + 12
y = 1/2 x - 7

D. y = 5/6 x + 3
y = -6/5 x - 2

Practice: Write the equation of the line that passes through the given point and is parallel to the given line (in point slope form).

1. (0, 5) y = 3x + 2
2. (-2, 4) y = 2x - 1
3. (1, -2) y = -4x + 3 - 3x
4. (1, -3) 4x + 2y = 8
5. (3, 6) 3y - 9x = 18
6. (-7, 0) -2x + 5y = 8x + 25

Practice Answers:
1. m = 3, y - 5 = 3 (x - 0)
2. m = 2, y - 4 = 2 (x + 2)
3. m = -7, y + 2 = -7 (x - 1)
4. m = -2, y + 3 = -2 (x - 1)
5. m = 3, y - 6 = 3 (x - 3)
6. m = 2, y - 0 = 2 (x + 7)

Parallel and Perpendicular Lines

1. Write the equation in point slope form and slope intercept form of a line that passes through the given point and is **parallel** to the given line.

(3, 4) $2x + y = 12$

Step 1: Solve the given equation for y to get $y = mx + b$. The sole purpose of this is to find SLOPE.
From this equation, **m = -2**.
You now have a **point (3, 4)**,
and the **slope, m = -2**.

1. (3,4)

$$2x + y = 12$$
$$-2x \qquad -2x$$
$$y = -2x + 12$$
$$y = -2x + 12$$

$$y - y_1 = m(x - x_1)$$

$$y - 4 = -2(x - 3)$$

$$y - 4 = -2(x - 3)$$
$$y - 4 = -2x + 6$$
$$+4 \qquad +4$$
$$y = -2x + 10$$

Step 2: Plug in **m = -2** and the given point **(3, 4)** into **point slope form** $y - y_1 = m(x - x_1)$. *$y - 4 = -2(x - 3)$*

Step 3: Using the point slope form equation, simplify to find **slope intercept form** $y = mx + b$. *$y = -2x + 10$*

---

2. Write the equation in point slope form and slope intercept form of a line that passes through the given point and is **perpendicular** to the given line.

(3, 4) $2x + y = 12$

1. (3,4)

$$2x + y = 12$$
$$-2x \qquad -2x$$
$$y = -2x + 12$$
$$y = -2x + 12$$

$$y - y_1 = m(x - x_1)$$

$$y - 4 = \frac{1}{2}(x - 3)$$

$$y - 4 = \frac{1}{2}(x - 3)$$
$$y - 4 = \frac{1}{2}x + \frac{3}{2}$$
$$+4 \qquad +\frac{4}{1} \cdot \frac{2}{2} = \frac{8}{2}$$
$$y = \frac{1}{2}x + \frac{11}{2}$$

$$y = \frac{1}{2}x + \frac{11}{2}$$

Perpendicular = −(flip)

$$m = -2 \rightarrow -\left(\frac{1}{-2}\right) \rightarrow \frac{-1}{-2} = \frac{1}{2}$$

Step 1: Solve the given equation for y to get $y = mx + b$. The purpose of this is to find SLOPE.
From this equation, **m = -2**.
You have a **point (3, 4)**,
and the **slope, m = -2**.
The slope PERPENDICULAR to m = -2 is **m = + 1/2**. [*opposite sign, reciprocal*]

Step 2: Plug in **m = 1/2** and the given point **(3, 4)** into **point slope form** $y - y_1 = m(x - x_1)$. *$y - 4 = \frac{1}{2}(x - 3)$*

Step 3: Using the point slope form equation, simplify to find **slope intercept form** $y = mx + b$. *$y = \frac{1}{2}x + \frac{11}{2}$*

Practice: Write the equation of the line that passes through the given point and is perpendicular to the given line. (in point slope form).

1. (0, 5) $y = -2x - 1$
2. (-2, 4) $y = \frac{1}{3}x + 1$
3. (1, -2) $y = 4x + 5 - 6x$
4. (1, -3) $-3x + 2y = 10$
5. (3, 6) $4y - 8x = 16$
6. (-7, 0) $-x + 3y = 8x + 4$

Practice Answers:
1. $m = \frac{1}{2},\ y - 5 = \frac{1}{2}(x - 0)$
2. $m = -3,\ y - 4 = -3(x + 2)$
3. $m = \frac{1}{2},\ y + 2 = \frac{1}{2}(x - 1)$
4. $m = \frac{-2}{3},\ y + 3 = \frac{-2}{3}(x - 1)$
5. $m = \frac{-1}{2},\ y - 6 = \frac{-1}{2}(x - 3)$
6. $m = \frac{-1}{3},\ y - 0 = \frac{-1}{3}(x + 7)$

Inequalities, ± Equations

The alligator always eats the **BIGGER VALUE!**

$x < 5$ *x is less than 5*	**$x > 5$** *x is greater than 5*
$2 < 5$ *2 is less than 5*	**$1 \leq a \leq 4$** *a is greater than or = to 1, and less than or = to 4*
$-3 \leq y < 8$ *y is greater than or = to -3 and less than 8*	

Solving inequality equations using ADDITION and SUBTRACTION

Solving inequality equations is just like solving regular equations. The only difference is that inequalities give a large range of answers, for example *x > 5 means that x can be ANY NUMBER greater than 5*. Whereas, *x = 5 means that x ONLY = 5.*

A.
$x + 3 < 5$
$x + 3 < 5$
$\quad -3 \quad -3$
$x < 2$
$x < 2$

B.
$x - 2 > 14$
$x - 2 > 14$
$\quad +2 \quad +2$
$x > 16$
$x > 16$

C.
$18 \leq -4 + x$
$-18 \leq -4 + x$
$+4 \quad +4$
$-14 \leq x$
$x \geq -14$

D.
$6x + 4 < 5x - 8$
$6x + 4 < 5x - 8$
$\quad -4 \quad -4$
$6x < 5x - 12$
$-5x \quad -5x$
$1x < -12$
$x < -12$

Check the answers. Plug in a value for x that fits the answer.

$x = 1$
$x + 3 < 5$
$1 + 3 < 5$
$4 < 5$
TRUE ✓

$x = 18$
$x - 2 > 14$
$18 - 2 > 14$
$16 > 14$
TRUE ✓

$x = -12$
$-18 \leq -4 + x$
$-18 \leq -4 + (-12)$
$-18 \leq -16$
TRUE ✓

$x = -15$
$6x + 4 < 5x - 8$
$6(-15) + 4 < 5(-15) - 8$
$-90 + 4 < -75 - 8$
$-86 < -83$
TRUE ✓

All answers are TRUE, therefore, correct.

Practice: Solve the following inequalities.

1. $x - 3 > 15$
2. $x + 4 < -10$
3. $15 \leq 5 + x$
4. $x + 7 \geq 8$
5. $7x - 3 < 6x + 5$
6. $-10 \geq x - 2$
7. $8 + x \leq 12$
8. $10x + 5 > 9x - 6$

Practice Answers:

1. $x > 18$ 2. $x < -14$ 3. $x \geq 10$ 4. $x \geq 1$ 5. $x < 8$ 6. $x \leq -8$ 7. $x \leq 4$ 8. $x > -11$

More practice: Algebra Is Easy Part 1 SUCCESS BOOK (Workbook + Test Book)

Inequalities, x/÷ Equations

Solving inequality equations using MULTIPLICATION and DIVISION

Multiply and divide just as in a regular equation. Whatever operation you do on one side, you must do on the other.

A.
$$6x < 54$$
$$\frac{6x}{6} < \frac{54}{6}$$
$$x < 9$$

B.
$$3x \leq -12$$
$$\frac{3x}{3} \leq \frac{-12}{3}$$
$$x \leq -4$$

C.
$$\frac{x}{4} \geq -5$$
$$4 \cdot \frac{x}{4} \geq -5 \cdot 4$$
$$x \geq -20$$

D.
$$\frac{3}{2}x < 9$$
$$\frac{2}{3} \cdot \frac{3}{2}x < \frac{9}{1} \cdot \frac{2}{3}$$
$$x < \frac{18}{3}$$
$$x < 6$$

SPECIAL CASE, switch direction of inequality

The direction of the inequality will switch ONLY if a negative is multiplied or divided ACROSS the inequality.

E.
$$-5x > -20$$
$$\frac{-5x}{-5} > \frac{-20}{-5}$$
$$x < 4$$

F.
$$-\frac{4}{5}x \leq 8$$
$$\left(-\frac{5}{4}\right) -\frac{4}{5}x \leq 8\left(-\frac{5}{4}\right)$$
$$x \geq -\frac{40}{4}$$
$$x \geq -10$$

G.
$$2 - x < 4$$
$$2 - x - 2 < 4 - 2$$
$$\frac{-x}{-1} < \frac{4}{-1}$$
$$x > -4$$

Example 7: If you have a (- x), you must multiply by -1 or divide by -1 to make the x positive. The final answer cannot have a negative sign in front of the variable.

Written by April Chloe Terrazas

Practice: Solve the following inequalities.

1. $\frac{2}{3}x > 12$
2. $5x < -15$
3. $25 \leq \frac{1}{2}x$
4. $-8x \geq 64$
5. $\frac{5}{2}x < 15$
6. $-10 \geq 2x$
7. $-\frac{3}{4}x \leq 12$
8. $5 - x > 7$

Practice Answers:

1. $x > 18$ 2. $x < -3$ 3. $x \geq 50$ 4. $x \leq -8$ 5. $x < 6$ 6. $x \leq -5$ 7. $x \geq -16$ 8. $x \leq -2$

Inequalities, Multi-Step Equations

Multi-step inequality equations are JUST LIKE regular equations, except you have to watch for **multiplying and dividing by negatives** as that will **change the direction of the inequality**.

A.

$$\boxed{5x + 8 \geq 3(4x + 6)}$$

$$5x + 8 \geq 3(4x + 6)$$
$$5x + 8 \geq 12x + 18$$
$$-5x \qquad -5x$$
$$8 \geq 7x + 18$$
$$-18 \qquad -18$$
$$-10 \geq 7x$$
$$\frac{-10}{7} \geq \frac{7x}{7}$$
$$-\frac{10}{7} \geq x$$

same

$$\boxed{x \leq -\frac{10}{7}}$$

Step 1: distribute 3 to (4x + 6)
Step 2: subtract 5x from left side, then right side
Step 3: subtract 18 from right side, then left side
Step 4: divide by 7 on right side, then left side
Rewrite answer so x is written first.

B.

$$\boxed{-3(2x + 5) < -18x}$$

$$-3(2x + 5) < -18x$$
$$-6x - 15 < -18x$$
$$+6x \qquad +6x$$
$$-15 < -12x$$
$$\frac{-15}{-12} \qquad \frac{-12x}{-12}$$

$$\frac{-15 \div 3}{-12 \div 3} = \frac{5}{4}$$

$$\frac{5}{4} > x$$

same

$$\boxed{x < \frac{5}{4}}$$

Step 1: distribute -3 to (2x + 5)
Step 2: add 6x to left side, then right side
Step 3: **divide by -12** on right side, then left side
Step 4: reduce -15/-12 and **FLIP the inequality**
Rewirte answer so x is written first.

Practice: Solve the following multi-step inequalities.

1. $-4(x - 3) < 15$
2. $3x + 4 \geq 3(2x - 1)$
3. $11 + 4(x + 1) \leq 5 + x$
4. $x - 12 \geq 8(x + 2)$
5. $3x + 3 + 4x < 6x - 1$
6. $-5(2x + 3) \geq 4x - 1$

Practice Answers: *1. $x > -3/4$* *2. $x \leq 7/3$* *3. $x \leq -10/3$* *4. $x \leq -4$* *5. $x < -4$* *6. $x \leq -1$*

Compound Inequalities

As in any equation, the objective is to solve for x (or the variable)
In compound inequalities, you must repeat the operation on EITHER SIDE of the inequalities.
Whatever is done in the middle section to get x by itself, must also be done on **both the left and right sides.**

A.

$$-3 < 5 + 2x \leq 25$$

$$-3 < 5 + 2x \leq 25$$

$$\begin{array}{ccccc} -3 & < & 5 + 2x & \leq & 25 \\ ② -5 & & ① -5 & & -5 ③ \\ \hline -8 & < & 2x & \leq & 20 \\ ⑤ \overline{2} & & ④ \overline{2} & & \overline{2} ⑥ \end{array}$$

$$-4 < x \leq 10$$

Step 1-3: subtract 5 from the MIDDLE, then left, then right
Whatever is done in the middle section
MUST BE DONE ON BOTH
THE LEFT AND RIGHT SIDES!
Step 4-6: divide by 2 in the MIDDLE, then left, then right.

This means x can be any value greater than -4 and less than or = to 10. *For example, x = -3.5, -2, -1, 0, 4, 7, 10 are all answers.*

B.

$$-5 \leq 7 - 3x < 25$$

$$-5 \leq 7 - 3x < 25$$

$$\begin{array}{ccccc} -5 & \leq & 7 - 3x & < & 25 \\ ② -7 & & ① -7 & & ③ -7 \\ \hline -12 & \leq & -3x & < & 18 \\ ⑤ \overline{-3} & & ④ \overline{-3} & & ⑥ \overline{-3} \end{array}$$

$$4 \geq x > -6$$

$$-6 < x \leq 4$$

same

Step 1-3: subtract 7 from the MIDDLE, then left, then right.
Whatever is done in the middle section
MUST BE DONE ON BOTH
THE LEFT AND RIGHT SIDES!
Step 4-6: **divide by -3** in the MIDDLE, then left, then right, and **FLIP the inequality signs.**
Rewrite the answer so less on left, greater on right.

Written by April Chloe Terrazas

Practice: Solve the following compound inequalities.

1. $-4 < x - 3 < 15$
2. $8 < x + 4 < 10$
3. $-20 \leq 5 + x < 13$
4. $23 < 4x + 7 \leq 35$
5. $2 < 3x - 7 < 5$
6. $-4 \leq -2(x - 1) \leq 18$

Practice Answers: 1. $-1 < x < 18$ 2. $4 < x < 6$ 3. $-25 \leq x < 8$ 4. $4 < x \leq 7$ 5. $3 < x < 4$ 6. $-8 \leq x \leq 3$

Absolute Value Inequalities

Review Absolute Value equations on p. 32 before you begin. The same principles apply to inequalities. Example A is the same as p. 32 only this time, it is an inequality.

A. $3|2x+6|-7 \le 5$

$+7 \quad +7$

$3|2x+6| \le 12$

$\div 3 \quad \div 3$

$|2x+6| \le 4$ — 2 equations

$2x+6 \le +4$	$2x+6 \ge -4$
$2x+6 \le 4$	$2x+6 \ge -4$
$-6 \quad -6$	$-6 \quad -6$
$2x \le -2$	$2x \ge -10$
$\frac{2x}{2} \le \frac{-2}{2}$	$\frac{2x}{2} \ge \frac{-10}{2}$
$x \le -1$	$x \ge -5$

Ex A. NOTE: When making **2 equations** to solve, the first has the same inequality (**≤**) and the same value (**+ 4**).
The second equation has the opposite inequality (**≥**) and the opposite value (**- 4**).

$x \le -1$
$x \ge -5$

can be re-written like this:
$-5 \le x \le -1$

x can be any value between -5 and -1.

Check any value in the interval from -5 to -1 and the answer will be TRUE if it is correct.

This checked for x = -2.

The end of the check 2 ≤ 4 is true, therefore the answer is correct.

$3|2(-2)+6|-7 \le 5$
$3|-4+6|-7 \le 5$
$3|2|-7 \le 5$
$+7 \quad +7$
$3|2| \le 12$
$\div 3 \quad \div 3$
$|2| \le 4$
$2 \le 4$ ✓

B. $|2x-3| > 5$

$2x-3 > 5$	$2x-3 < -5$
$2x-3 > 5$	$2x-3 < -5$
$+3 \quad +3$	$+3 \quad +3$
$2x > 8$	$2x < -2$
$\frac{2x}{2} > \frac{8}{2}$	$\frac{2x}{2} < \frac{-2}{2}$
$x > 4$	$x < -1$

$x \le -1 \quad x \ge -5$

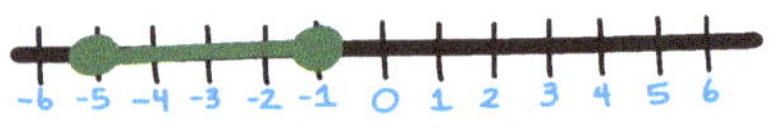

$-5 \le x \le -1$

$x < -1 \quad x > 4$

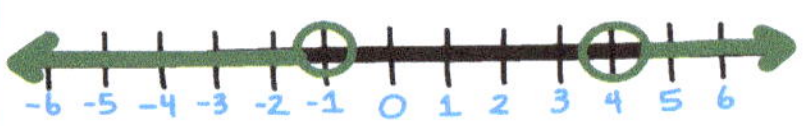

Graphing on a number line REVIEW:
Filled Circle ≤ or ≥
Hollow Circle < or >

Basic Inequality, one value
Compound Inequality, two values

Basic

$x < 2$

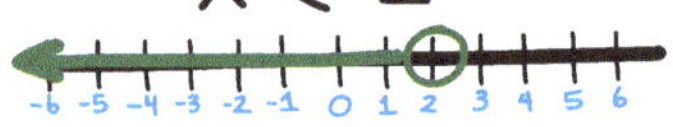

$x \le 2$

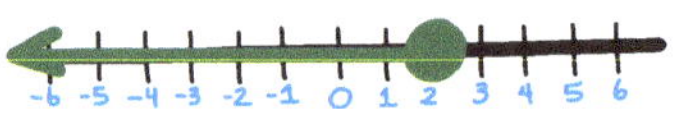

Compound

$-3 < x \le 4$

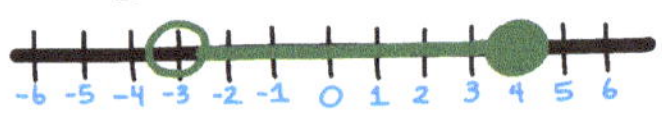

$x \le -2 \qquad x > 0$

More practice: Algebra Is Easy Part 1 SUCCESS BOOK (Workbook + Test Book)

Absolute Value Inequalities Practice

Practice: Solve the following inequalities.

1. $|x| < 3$
2. $|x+2| \leq -5$
3. $|3x| > 15$
4. $|2x - 3| \geq 7$
5. $2|x + 4| > 10$
6. $3|2x + 5| \leq 12$
7. $5|4x - 3| + 2 \geq 17$
8. $|8x - 10| < 14$

9. Graph the following basic inequalities on a number line:

a. $x > 4$ b. $x < -3$ c. $x \leq 0$ d. $x \geq -1$ e. $x > 5$

10. Graph the following compound inequalities on a number line:

a. $-5 < x < 2$ b. $x < -2, x \geq 3$ c. $2 \leq x < 4$ d. $x \leq -1, x \geq 5$ e. $-3 < x < 6$

Written by April Chloe Terrazas

11. Label the following graphs with the correct inequality:

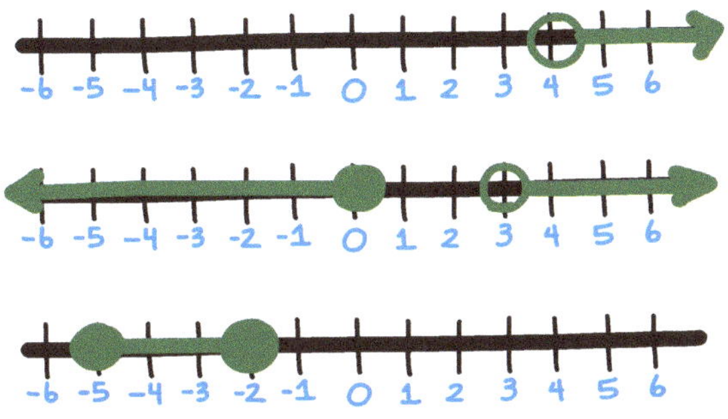

Practice Answers: 1. $x > -3, x < 3$ or $3 < x < 3$
2. $x \leq -7, x \geq 3$ 3. $x < -5$ and $x > 5$
4. $x \geq 5, x \leq -2$ 5. $x < -9, x > 1$
6. $x \leq -1/2, x \geq -9/2$ 7. $x \leq 0, x \geq 3/2$
8. $x < 3, x > -1/2$
11. $x > 4$, $x \leq 0$ and $x > 3$, $-5 \leq x \leq -2$

9.
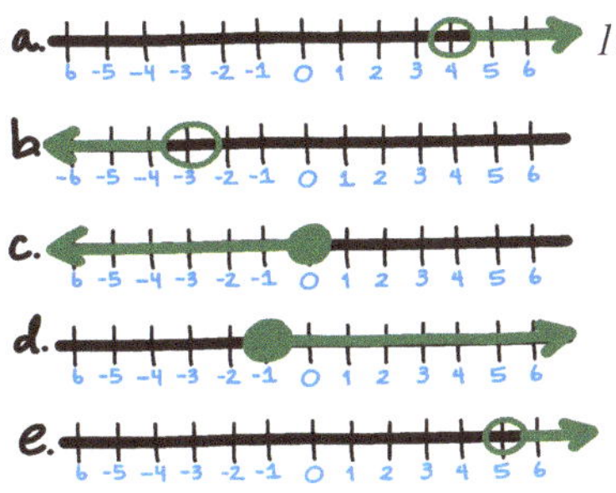

10.
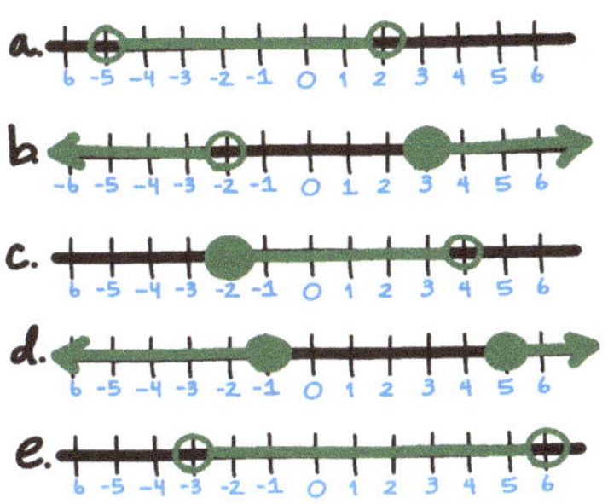

Graphing Inequalities on a Grid

$<$ or $>$ the LINE IS DASHED. - - - - - - - -

$\leq$ or $\geq$ the LINE IS SOLID. ————

If $>$ or $\geq$, shade ABOVE THE LINE (on the positive side)

If $<$ or $\leq$, shade BELOW THE LINE (on the negative side)

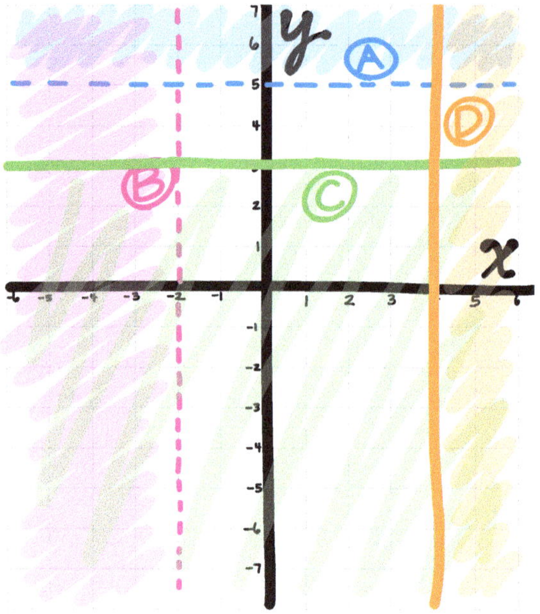

A. **$y > 5$** dashed horizontal line at $y = 5$
shade above the line

B. **$x < -2$** dashed vertical line at $x = -2$
shade below (or left) the line

C. **$y \leq 3$** solid horizontal line at $y = 3$
shade below the line

D. **$x \geq 4$** solid vertical line at $x = 4$
shade above (or right) the line

E. **$y > 2x + 1$** dashed line, shade above

F. **$y \leq -\frac{1}{3}x - 5$** solid line, shade below

G. $3x + 5y > 6x - 10$ *solve for y*

$$\begin{aligned} 3x + 5y &> 6x - 10 \\ -3x \quad &\quad -3x \\ \frac{5y}{5} &> \frac{3x}{5} - \frac{10}{5} \end{aligned}$$

$y > \frac{3}{5}x - 2$ dashed line, shade above

<u>Linear Equation VS Linear INequality</u>

A linear equality is a solid line and any POINT on that line is a solution. (Ex: $y = 2x + 1$)

A linear INequality is an entire AREA on a graph and any point in the shaded AREA is a solution. (Ex: $y \leq 2x + 1$)

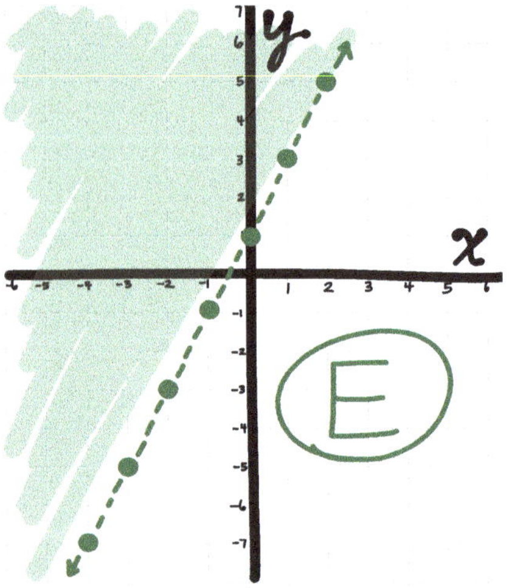

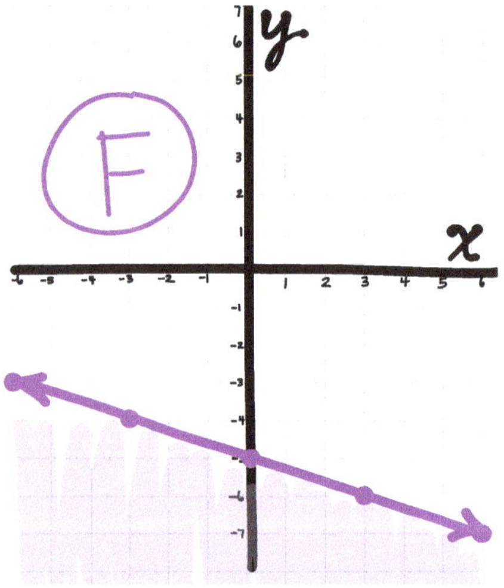

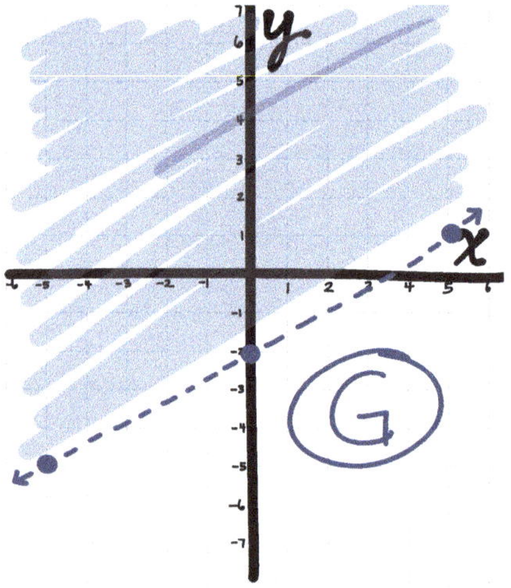

The solution to an inequality can be found anywhere in the shaded area.

In example E, solutions are (-5, 0), (1, 4), (-3, -1) + more! No point along the line is a solution (it is dashed).

In example F, solutions are (0, -5), (4, -7), (-5, -6) + more, also any point on the line (it is a solid line).

In example G, solutions are (0, 0), ((-1, 5), (-5, -1) + more! No point along the line is a solution (it is dashed).

If there are multiple lines being graphed together, the solution lies in the CROSSOVER shaded area.

More practice: Algebra Is Easy Part 1 SUCCESS BOOK (Workbook + Test Book)

Graphing Inequalities on a Grid

Practice. Graph the following inequalities:

1. $y < 2x - 3$

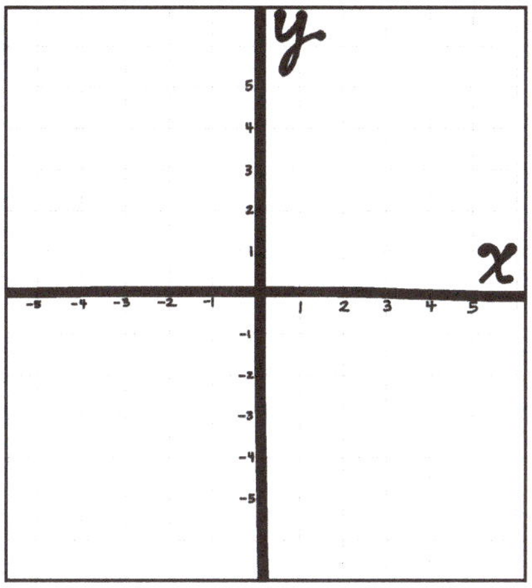

2. $y \geq -1/3\,x + 4$

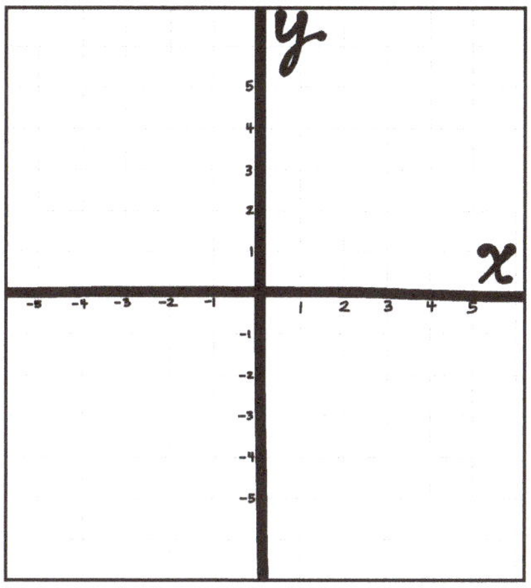

3. $4x + 6y > -12$

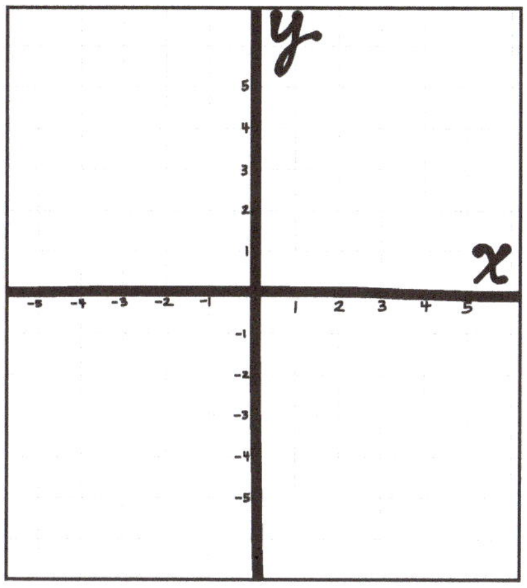

4. $x < -2$ and $y > 1$

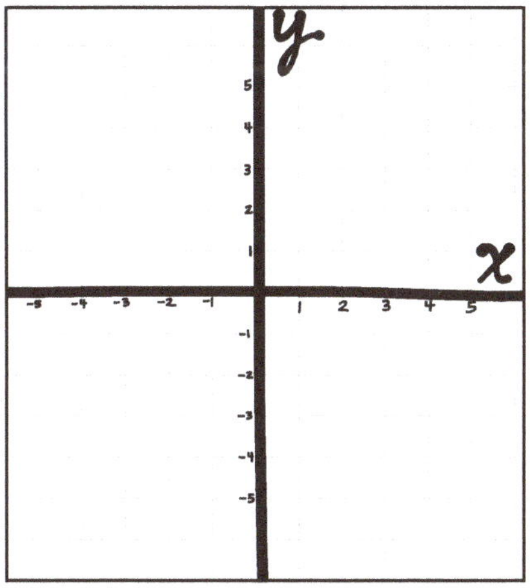

5. $8x - 4y \leq 20$

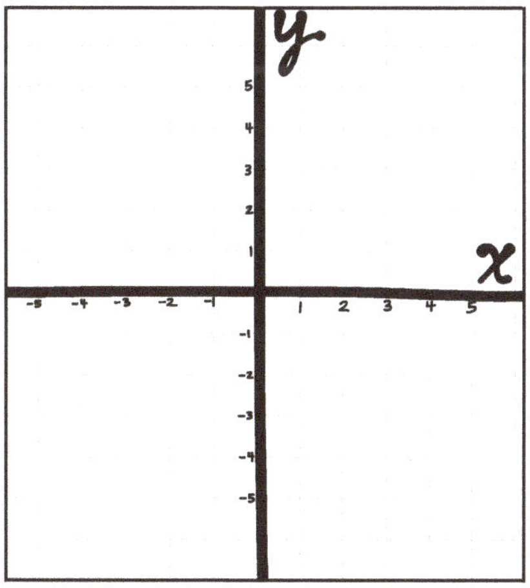

6. $y \leq -2$ and $x > 2$

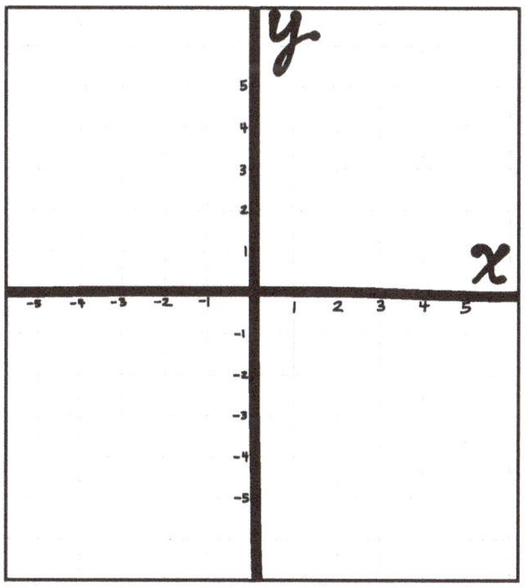

Practice Answers:

1.
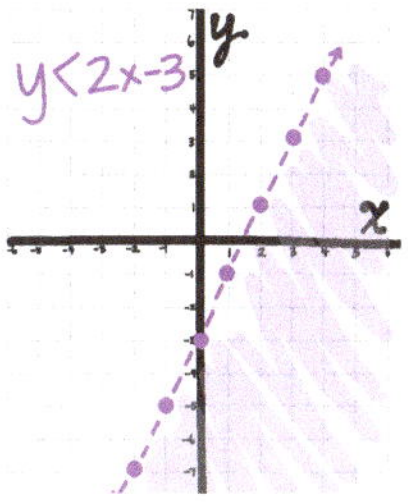

2.
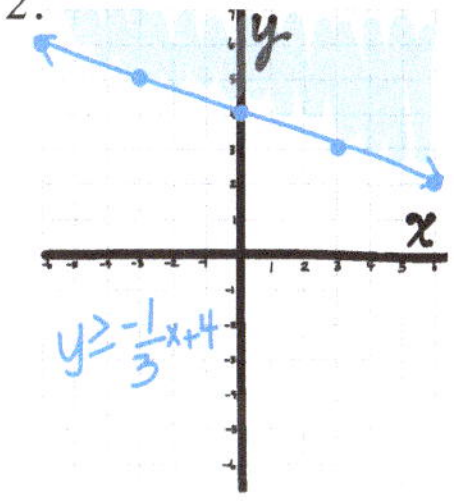

3.
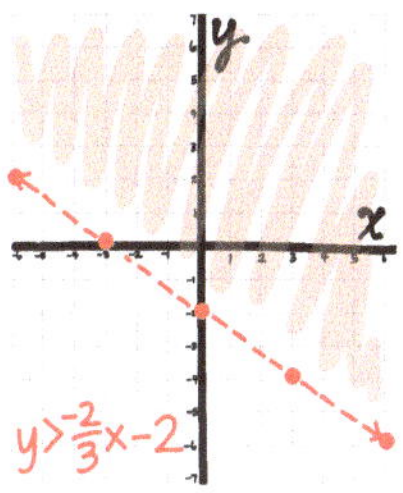

4.
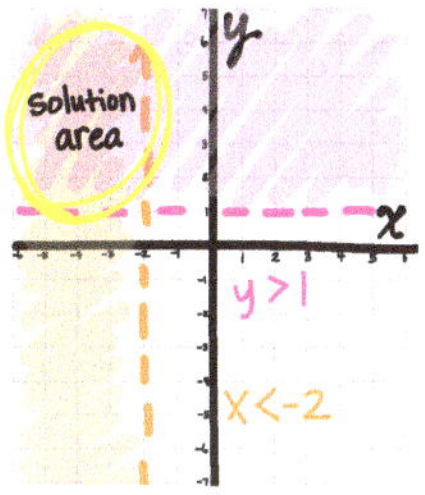

5.
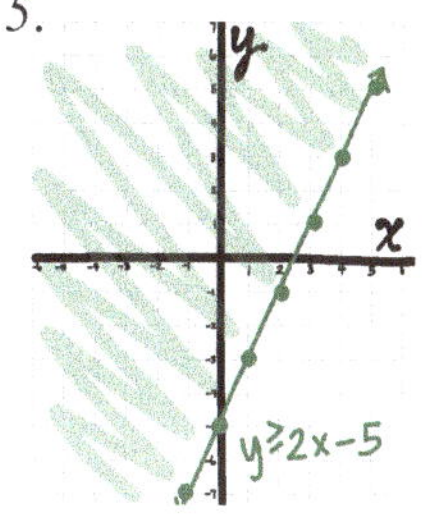

6.
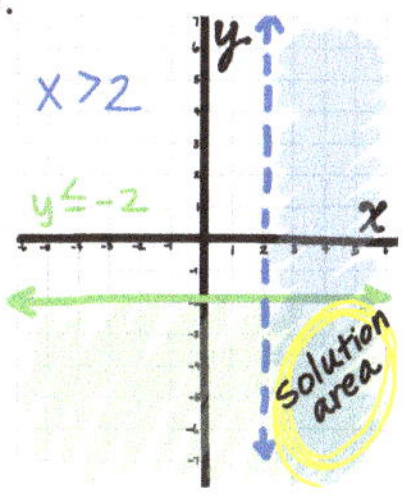

EXCELLENT WORK SO FAR!!!

Continue with Algebra is Easy Part 2.

Remember to use ALL of the resources we have for Algebra 1!

Algebra is Easy Part 1

Algebra is Easy Part 2

Algebra is Easy ***SUCCESS BOOK*** Part 1 & Part 2

Algebra is Easy ***FULL BOOK WEBINAR*** Part 1 & Part 2

all available at www.Crazy-Brainz.com.

Other books in the MATH IS EASY Series:
Geometry is Easy
Algebra 2 is Easy
Pre-Calculus is Easy

Middle School Math is Easy
Elementary School Math is Easy

The GED is Easy
The SAT is Easy

www.ingramcontent.com/pod-product-compliance
Lightning Source LLC
LaVergne TN
LVHW070834080426
835508LV00031B/3461
* 9 7 8 1 9 4 1 7 7 5 2 5 7 *